The Boobie Boys

Murder and Mayhem in Miami

Tony Monheim

DEDICATION

As always, for Nancy.

In Memory of Major Tyrone White
May 29, 1961 - September 20, 2020

Thou Shalt Not Kill.
-Exodus 20:13

Remember, we work for God.
-Homicide Commander Vernon Geberth

There is no hunting like the hunting of
man, and those who have hunted armed
men long enough and liked it, never care
for anything else thereafter.
-Ernest Hemingway

ACKNOWLEDGMENTS

Cover designed by:
Det. Steve Zimmerman MDPD Homicide
(ret.)

Thanks for the commas (and the tenses),
Julie!

And many thanks to my beta reader, Pat
Walton.

Author's Note

What you are about to read is true. This account has been chronicled as faithfully as possible from tens of thousands of pages of police reports, court documents, news articles, and personal notes.

Pat Conroy, the author of *The Great Santini* and *The Prince of Tides*, once said that when we pick up a book and open it, we are simply asking the writer to "tell us a story." Well, this is one heck of a story.

Part One

CHAPTER 1
Gerry Dukes

March 17, 1994

St. Patrick's Day! It was nearly the end of my shift, and I was eagerly looking forward to a green beer at the PBA lounge. But it was not to be. At 10:40 p.m., my homicide squad received word that two men had been gunned down in the parking lot of a Carol City shopping center. One of the victims, 23-year-old Gerry Dukes, was dead at the scene. The second victim, John Hankins, had been taken to Golden Glades Hospital in critical condition.

Even though we left the Homicide office in separate vehicles, my squad and I arrived at the strip shopping plaza just north of 183rd Street on NW 42nd Avenue, at about the same time. As we pulled up to the intersection, we could see spent shell casings scattered all over the parking lot. It looked like a war zone.

I climbed out of my unmarked white

Ford Tempo and walked toward the yellow police tape that encircled the shopping center. A young burglary detective from the Northwest District named Ken Ottley lifted the tape above his head and allowed me to enter the crime scene.

"You've got two victims, Sarge. One was taken to the hospital in bad shape, and the other one is behind that building over there," he said pointing.

I squatted down to try and determine what type of cartridges had been used. They were 7.62x39 center-fire bottleneck rounds that had originated in Soviet Russia and were used primarily in SKS and AK-47 weapons.

Just as the Thompson .45 caliber machine gun had become the weapon of choice during the gangland wars in Al Capone's Chicago, the AK-47 was now the preferred armament of the drug gangs that operated in South Florida.

The "AK" stands for Automatic Kalashnikov (Avtomat Kalashnikova) and the "47" designates the year that it was first mass produced for the Russian army. The design was created by a Russian gunsmith (and later General in the Russian Army) named Mikhail Kalashnikov. The seventeenth of nineteen children, Kalashnikov was what he called a "tinkerer" all his life. He was conscripted into the Red Army and in 1941, was severely wounded in combat. He spent six months recovering in a military hospital where he heard countless complaints from his fellow injured soldiers who grumbled about the unreliability of the rifles they had been issued. They were distressed that the weapons constantly jammed.

As soon as he was discharged from the hospital, he began working on the prototype of what would become the famous AK-47, that chambered the newly developed 7.62x39 cartridge. Seven decades later, it is still one of the most popular and widely used rifles in the world. But although the AK is a superb weapon, it is the 7.62 round that makes it so devastating. The projectile enters small and exits large, causing enormous amounts of tissue damage along its path.

During an interview, Kalashnikov said that he designed the rifle to critically wound the enemy and not necessarily kill him because he felt that this would take three enemy soldiers out of the battle.... the one who was severely injured and the two others who had to drag him from the battlefield.

Both the AK-47 and the SKS rifles made their debut in the Miami drug culture during the late 80s and the results were catastrophic. They were, and still are, used to enforce, intimidate, and retaliate. Their awesome firepower has been used to kill and maim hundreds of individuals in South Florida, some of them completely innocent children who became collateral damage in the never-ending drug wars.

Two crime lab technicians began photographing the scene and documenting the evidence. They would eventually impound 99 shell casings from the parking lot, most of them 7.62x39. Twenty of the casings were determined to be .223 caliber.

The .223 is also a centerfire, bottle-necked cartridge that was developed in 1957 by the Remington Arms Company. It is used in the M-16, the Colt AR-15, the Ruger mini-14, the Heckler and Koch 630, and a variety of other long guns.

The shooting occurred on the west side of the Oasis barber shop. An eyewitness who worked for the U.S. Postal service as a letter carrier said he was in the barber shop with Dukes, Hankins, and the shop's owner, Zeus Wilson, just prior to the gunfire.

The barber shop doubled as a beeper store. In 1994, cell phones weren't as ubiquitous as they are today. Beepers and pay phones were state-of-the-art communications devices back then, and in the early 90s they had become a staple for drug dealers plying their trade. In an article in the Los Angeles Times during that era, reporter Paul Lieberman noted that "for today's criminal organizations, beepers are more important tools than guns or getaway cars."

In 1990, the DEA estimated that 90% of

all narcotics transactions were conducted using beepers and pay phones. Pay phones are nearly non-existent today but in the early 90s they were on every corner in most urban areas.

Criminals have always been on the forefront of technology, and by 1994 even though the cell phone was gaining popularity in the underworld as an efficient way to communicate, pagers were still very popular. So, when it was learned that Zeus Wilson was running a beeper store in his barber shop, this raised an obvious red flag.

I interviewed the mail carrier witness and he said he had gotten to the barber shop around 10 p.m. Dukes and Hankins were already there when he arrived. Zeus gave all three of them haircuts, and at a little after 10:30, he announced that he was closing for the evening. Gerry Dukes smiled at the others and said, "I've been here for hours; they might know I'm here, and I might get shot leaving." His words would certainly become prophetic.

The mail carrier recounted what happened next:

All four of us was in the parking lot. Zeus was carrying a big bag full of beepers and was trying to lock the door to the shop. Duke had just turned the alarm off on his car and 'Six' (Hankins's nickname) was getting in the passenger side. I was walking to my car; I had told Zeus I would give him a ride home. When I looked back, I saw two guys with big guns getting out of a car and walking toward Duke. Duke is a big dope boy, so I figured they was coming for him. They didn't say nothin' and just started shootin'.

Dukes was standing beside his 1987 Sterling[1] when the two shooters unleashed a furious barrage of gunfire. He tried to flee to the rear of the shopping center but was mowed down. The shooter with the AK-47 strafed his body repeatedly with gunfire.

The witness continued his narrative:

When the shootin' started I just ran toward the

---

[1] The Sterling was manufactured in the United Kingdom and sold in the United States from 1987 -1991. Only 14,000 were sold in the U.S in 1987.

Shell Station. I looked back and seen them killin' Duke while he was on the ground. It seemed like the shootin' went on forever. Then I seen them get into a black car, maybe a Hyundai or something like that. I looked to get the license tag number, but it ain't have no tag on it. They took off north on 42nd Avenue with no lights on.

When he returned to his car in the parking lot, he saw that Hankins was badly wounded. "Six was shot up real bad, in his arms and his legs and his face. I put him in my car and took him straight to the hospital," the witness said.

I asked him if he saw the gunmen's faces and if he could identify them if he saw them again. "No," he said. "I was too scared."

Detective Bob Singer contacted the Medical Examiner's Office from a pay phone at the nearby Shell gas station and requested that the on-call ME respond.

"Dr. Barnhart[2] will be enroute," he said

---

[2] Dr. Jay Barnhart started as family doctor in the Chesapeake Bay area of Maryland when he graduated from medical

as he handed me a piece of paper with the ME's case number on it.

The doctor arrived 55 minutes later. We all accompanied him to where Dukes lay face up in a grassy area near the building. He was a mess. His head, torso, legs, and arms were mangled and mutilated by the over forty projectiles that had torn through his body.

"What do you think, doc?" I asked.

He looked at me. "Well, I can confirm that he's dead," he said with no trace of humor in his voice. "There's not much to work with here, is there?"

Detective Jay Vas leaned over with his hands on his knees and examined the body more closely. "I don't think I've ever seen a body shot up this bad, not even in 'Nam."

This was a profound statement,

---

school. He had a thriving practice, delivering babies and making house calls, but after 17 years he made a dramatic career change…. he decided he wanted to become a Medical Examiner. At the age of 45 he went back to medical school for four years and did a one-year residency. He and his wife moved to Miami where he became an Associate Medical Examiner. He served in that capacity for nearly 20 years until he retired. Today he is an accomplished pianist who plays professionally with a repertoire of over a thousand songs.

especially coming from Jay. He had served three tours of duty in Vietnam as a Green Beret. He was wounded four times; the last time was nearly fatal. He was shipped back to his hometown in Iowa, and while he was recovering, he was awarded the Bronze Star and a Purple Heart with two Oak Leaf Clusters. He was fully acquainted with the AK-47 and the destructive effects it could have on the human body.

Figure 1. 1987 Sterling driven by Gerry Dukes. Note the bullet holes. (Author)

The ME and the crime lab finished their work and, by 1 a.m. all the gawkers who had lined up along the yellow police tape had lost interest and walked away.

The only piece of evidence left at the crime scene to be impounded was the dead body of Gerry Dukes. I stood in the parking lot with my team of detectives as we sipped coffee waiting for the arrival of the Medical Examiner's wagon to transport the corpse.

It was a cool night, and except for an occasional passing car, it had become eerily quiet. We were all suddenly startled by the loud cracks of automatic weapons fire just to the east of our location.

"That was close," Bob said, as we all instinctively scurried for cover behind the wall of the nearby building.

We would later learn that 19-year-old Bennie Brownlee had been killed in a hail of bullets, just three blocks away in retaliation for the murder of Gerry Dukes.

CHAPTER 2
Boobie

The next morning, after a few hours of sleep, I grabbed a cup of coffee and trudged into my garage. I rummaged through some of the clutter looking for an old sieve I had made years earlier to sift small rocks out of my kids' sandbox. I eventually found it behind a stack of lumber. It was a simple wooden frame with a wire mesh screen attached to the bottom. I tossed it, along with a long-handled shovel, into the trunk of my Tempo and headed to the Carol City shopping center. As I drove, I got on the radio and requested that a crime lab unit meet me there.

Mike Melgarejo was getting out of his green and white crime scene van when I pulled into the parking lot. I took the shovel and sieve from my trunk and walked to where Gerry Dukes' body was lying the night before. I explained to Mike that I wanted to try and recover some of the projectiles from the ground. There was a large layer of dried crusted blood where the body had been, so I used the shovel to lift it up and toss it to the side. I took several shovelfuls of dirt and dumped them into the sieve. When we shook it back and forth, the sandy soil sifted through, and two copper jacketed projectiles remained on the screen. Mike took photographs, and we continued the process for the next half hour, finding three additional bullets. He placed them in white pill boxes and labeled them.

"Mike, could you do me a favor and get those to the firearms section right away?" I said.

Firearms identification is a sub-category of toolmark identification. It is defined as the process of analyzing the bullets and cartridge cases left at a crime scene to determine if they came from a particular firearm. No two firearms, even those of the same make and model, will produce the same unique marks on fired bullets and cartridge casings. This is because of the variations in the metal that occur during the manufacturing process of the weapon. These variations rarely change over time. Firearms that are recovered years later can be positively identified as having fired a specific bullet or casing. This is sometimes referred to as the "mechanical fingerprint" of the gun.

When a high-powered weapon such as an AK-47 fires a round, distinctive marks from the inside of the barrel are transferred to the projectile. As the firing pin strikes the primer, it leaves a unique mark that is unlike any other firing pin mark. Likewise, when the casing is extracted from the chamber and ejected from the weapon, the characteristics of the extractor marks and ejector marks are unique to that rifle.

All the shoveling and sifting Mike and I did would eventually pay off. One of the firearms examiners, Jess Galan, was able to match the projectiles we recovered to two other shootings.

Exactly one week before the Gerry Dukes murder, the AK-47 was used in the drive-by shootings of two people near the Miami Dolphins Stadium. They were both wounded but not severely.

On January 6, 1994, that same AK-47 was used in the attempted murder of Bernard Shaw and Margo Shaw. Both were struck by the gunfire. Bernard Shaw received the brunt of the attack. He was hit seven times and was in critical condition but managed to pull through. They were sitting in a vehicle in front of Oneika and Ronald Raye's house when the shooting occurred. Oneika Raye was the registered owner of the 1987 Sterling Gerry Dukes was driving the night he was killed.

Shortly after leaving the shopping center, my pager went off. I used a nearby pay phone to call the Homicide Office. The receptionist relayed a message from Detective Rodney Polite of the North Safe Streets Unit. He said he had information about the Dukes murder, so I drove to the Matchboxes on NW 199 Street and 37th Avenue.

The Matchboxes was a government housing project built in the 60s and run by HUD. The units were stacked on top of one another at right angles and looked like the boxes that held wooden matches; hence the name Matchbox projects. The true name of the complex has been lost to the ages.

Rapper Rick Ross hung out at the Matchboxes (before he became famous) while playing football at nearby Carol City High School. More about Ross later.

The U.S. Department of Housing and Urban Development (HUD) furnished the Safe Streets Unit with an office in the Matchboxes. It was tiny and cramped, but it was better than nothing. Detective Polite was seated behind an old metal desk piled high with paperwork.

"You know what's going on here, don't you? With all these killings and shootings?" he asked as I walked in the door.

I admitted that I didn't.

"It's a feud between Boobie's Boys and the Thomas Family."

"Who is Boobie?" I asked.

"Kenneth Williams!" he practically shouted, as if I should know.

This was the first time I had ever heard

the name Boobie or Kenneth Williams, but it would, most certainly, not be the last.

Figure 2. Kenneth "Boobie" Williams.

At the time of the Gerry Dukes murder, Kenneth Williams was in control of a muti-state narcotics organization that distributed hundreds of kilos of powdered cocaine and crack cocaine throughout Florida, and into Georgia, Virginia, North Carolina, and Pennsylvania.

Boobie's seemingly meteoric rise from street tough to drug lord began in the early 90s by ripping off local drug dealers for their product. He would either burglarize the homes and vehicles of known drug sellers or rob them directly at gunpoint. He quickly developed a reputation as being both fearless and ruthless.

One day while he was visiting his twin cousins, Leonard, and Lenard Brown (known as Bo and Nard) in the Matchboxes, he spotted an enormous opportunity. Drug sales in the Matchboxes were controlled by a man named Kenneth "Can Head" Hayes. Boobie perceived Can Head as weak and with the help of the Twins, he plotted the takeover of his organization. They blatantly robbed and beat up Can Head's dealers and stole their narcotics. When his forces tried to resist, Boobie and his minions did not hesitate to engage in shootouts with them, wounding several. Can Head did not have the stomach for a protracted all-out war, so he simply gave in and relinquished his hold on the Matchbox projects to Boobie.

The Matchboxes became Kenneth Williams's domain. The 24/7 sales of powdered cocaine and crack cocaine provided a steady and lucrative income with which Boobie could now grow his organization.

Those that knew him said that Williams acquired the nickname "Boobie" from his mother, Judy. She would call him "her little Boobie." The pet-name stuck throughout his childhood and into adulthood. Williams's mother died of a massive stroke when he was 11 years old, so he lived with various relatives and friends in the Carol City area while growing up.

Carol City is a neighborhood in what is now the city of Miami Gardens. In the 1990s, Carol City was unincorporated Miami-Dade County. The population in 1995 was 55,000, most of whom were Black or Hispanic. The crime rate was high, and it had numerous government housing projects within its confines.

Carol City is famous for the "Carol City Six" murders, which occurred in 1977. While robbing a dope house, John Errol Ferguson, Marvin Francois, and Bufford White tied up and shot eight people execution-style. Six victims died. Ferguson, Francois, and White were convicted and executed. It is remarkable that Buford White was merely the getaway driver. He never entered the house and shot no one. Nevertheless, he was executed in 1987.

During his middle school and high school years, Boobie became very close with the families of Ronald "Rollo" Raye and Bernard Shaw. Both Raye and Shaw would become trusted lieutenants in his burgeoning criminal organization. Eventually, other family members and friends from the neighborhood would start working for Boobie. The lure, of course, was money. The fealty of those in his operation was initially unwavering, but some of these loyalties eroded over time.

In 1987, at the age of 16, Kenneth Williams committed his first murder.[3] In a dispute over stolen automobile parts, Boobie shot three people near Buccaneer Park in North Miami Dade County. Gary Coley died on the scene and two other

---

[3] This is Kenneth Williams first arrest for murder, but rumors persist that there are others that precede Coley's death.

teenagers were hospitalized. Boobie was arrested and taken to Youth Hall. He was convicted of the murder but was designated a "Youthful Offender" and only served a four-year sentence. (In the 1980s, the Miami-Dade criminal justice system was overwhelmed and became known for routinely dispensing *in*justice). While he was locked up in juvenile detention, he met Efrain Casado who was known as "E-4." This chance meeting would create a coalition years later that produced one of the most violent drug gangs in the history of Miami-Dade County.

Within weeks of his release, Boobie took part in another killing. He and his mentor in the dope business, Graylin Kelly, ambushed two teenagers at the Burger King Restaurant on NW 54th Street in Miami. Damien McCoy,[4] 18, and Laverryton Smith 19, were in the drive-through lane when a dark blue Mitsubishi pulled alongside their vehicle. Kelly opened fire, killing McCoy and wounding

---

[4] The murder charges are dropped when Kelly is convicted for drug trafficking by the Feds.

Smith.

Three weeks later Kelly was arrested in Tallahassee during a drug bust. Seized in the raid was $100,000 and two pounds of crack cocaine. A newspaper article in the *Tallahassee Democrat* quoted a police detective who called it "one of the largest crack cocaine seizures in the city's history." Kelly was arrested for the murder of McCoy but even though several witnesses named Boobie as the driver, he was never charged.

In the early 90s, the price for a kilo of cocaine in Miami-Dade County hovered between $14,000 and $18,000. By "bringing it up the road" to areas outside of Miami, the price could double and even triple.[5] Knowing this, Boobie created a network of locations where he could not only deliver his product but also distribute it to maximize his profits. He employed couriers who transported the kilos to various locations, paying them $700 to

---

[5] A kilo of cocaine in Miami in 2023, costs anywhere between $21,000 and $22,000.

$1,000 per trip.

Sam Jones, Jr. was one of those couriers. A native of Foley, Alabama, Jones met Boobie through the sister of one of Boobies' associates. He began by transporting powdered cocaine (usually five kilos at a time) to Pensacola, Florida. For each trip he was paid $1,000. On the first few trips, Boobie accompanied him and introduced him to the local dealers who distributed the drugs.

For the next two years Jones made two to three trips a month. He estimated that he delivered over 150 kilos of cocaine for Boobie. The cocaine he transported, originally purchased for $16,000 per kilo, had a street value of $36,000 a kilo once it reached Pensacola. This translated into a net profit of over $2 million ($4 million in today's dollars) for simply "bringing it up the road."

Jones would sometimes team up with Larry Holland who was a para-paraplegic and confined to a wheelchair. His disability provided the perfect cover to avoid police scrutiny. Holland also made a dozen solo trips to Pensacola and Tallahassee for Boobie, transporting an estimated 60 kilos.

Jones and Holland preferred to use Ford Taurus sedans to transport the narcotics because they had an area in the engine compartment that could be used to hide the drugs. This compartment could easily conceal five individually wrapped kilos and up to $110,000 in cash on the return trips to Miami.

To avoid detection by police drug dogs, the plastic wrapped packages were covered with motor oil.[6] Jones was stopped several times by the Florida Highway Patrol, but their dogs were never able to detect the scent of the cocaine because of the motor oil. (Other couriers learned that if they smeared axle grease on the kilos, the dogs would not alert either. Boobie eventually outfitted the vehicles used by his couriers with a compartment over the gas tank. This method proved to be foolproof. None of his shipments were ever intercepted.)

Jones described Boobie as mild-

---

[6] From court testimony and interviews with Jones and Holland conducted by DEA agent Lenny Athas.

mannered and personable. He said he didn't curse and even quoted the scriptures. But there were times when he would reveal his violent side. He recalled one incident in the Matchboxes when Boobie became angry with one of his workers Jones knew only as "Fish Grease." Fish Grease had been shot months earlier and was still wearing a colostomy bag. He had committed an unknown blunder that displeased Boobie. Jones said Fish Grease screamed in pain as Boobie punched him repeatedly in the colostomy bag as punishment for his mistake.

When $80,000 was discovered missing from one of Boobie's stash houses he suspected Jones and sent two of his henchmen to Pensacola to kill him. He was shot multiple times and hospitalized but survived. After being discharged from the hospital he had no further dealings with Boobie and moved back to Alabama.[7] Jones was eventually arrested by the DEA and sentenced to 135 months in Federal prison.

---

[7] Interview with Sgt. Dave Simmons

As his network expanded, Boobie hired more couriers to deliver his product. He was soon transporting his drugs to Atlanta and Augusta, Georgia, Raleigh, North Carolina, and Jacksonville, Florida using assorted female drivers. Most of whom were strippers from local strip clubs.

His business model became multifaceted. The street sales in the Matchboxes, and two other housing projects he took over in Carol City, gave him a continuous cash flow. His couriers delivered drugs to locations outside of Miami-Dade County where he either sold the kilos outright for a substantial profit, or in some venues, distributed them by using his own people.

Miami being Miami, there was always a robust market for the sale of large quantities of cocaine to buyers who would take it to cities like New York, Chicago, Washington D.C., or Detroit. An investment of $34,000 for two kilos by these entrepreneurs could easily be turned into a small fortune.

But by far, Boobie's highest profit

margin came from dope rips. Out of town buyers were robbed regularly. Many were from New York and New Jersey, and most of them just simply "gave it up" when guns were pointed at them. He would also brazenly rob the stash houses of the local drug dealers he had conducted transactions with weeks, days, or even hours earlier.[8]

As might be expected, there were occasional reprisals for these misdeeds. When Ronald Raye and Bernard Shaw robbed a dealer who worked for Alex Harris, Harris shot Shaw in the leg. Shaw and Boobie retaliated by spraying Harris's townhouse with AK-47s, trying to kill him. A fusillade of over 40 rounds ripped into the two-story home. Before fleeing, they also firebombed his Mercedes Benz. Harris was not even home when the shooting and fire-bombing took place. His wife, Keisha, and her cousin were though, and reported the incident to the police. They were both unhurt but were terrified and severely traumatized.

---

[8] Court testimony of Jason Ortega. Ortega assisted in dozens of these robberies.

In the late 1980s the demand for crack cocaine exploded and an insatiable appetite for it continued into the 90s. Miami is the birthplace of crack in the United States. Caribbean immigrants taught Miami dealers the technique of converting powdered cocaine into crack, and it spread like wildfire to every American city.

Crack cocaine is highly addictive. Far more addictive than powdered cocaine. There is much speculation about how crack got its name, but the most plausible explanation is from the crackling sound it makes when it is burned in a pipe. Although the "high" from crack only lasts about 10 to 15 minutes, it is exponentially far more intense than powdered cocaine.

It is the delivery system that makes crack so seductive. Powdered cocaine cannot be smoked. Cocaine hydrochloride will not vaporize until it reaches 370ºF. The powder will burn up long before reaching that temperature, making it impractical for use in a pipe. Crack cocaine, however, requires a temperature of only 194ºF to vaporize, and when inhaled will reach the brain within seconds.

Crack resembles small, off-white, crystalline rocks. It is made by mixing powdered cocaine with water and baking soda (sometimes ammonia is used). The mixture is boiled until the free base cocaine floats to the top and forms a round "cookie." The cookie is then cut up into small pieces and sold. The process sounds easy, but there is a technique to it. Many who try it destroy tens of thousands of dollars in cocaine before perfecting the procedure. Boobie learned how to cook his own crack to increase his profits. Moreover, crack cookies are far easier to conceal and transport than kilos of powdered cocaine.

Boobie acquired his cocaine from a variety of sources. Wimon Nero, who was known as "Cujo", and his wife, Rena Rose, always had an ample supply. As did Michelle Feliciano, her brother, Pedro, and her husband, Orelvi, known as "Cuban Shorty." Together, they smuggled hundreds of kilos into the U.S. on speedboats from the Bahamas. They began selling 10 kilos at a time to Graylin Kelly who introduced them to Boobie. When Kelly was sent to Allenwood Federal Prison for the sale of cocaine and murder, Boobie became one of their main outlets. Ronald Raye, and Bernard Shaw would often make the exchanges of money for the kilos of cocaine on Boobie's behalf.

This arrangement ended abruptly when Boobie ripped off one of Cuban Shorty's couriers, named Ariel Barrios. Barrios had ten kilos hidden at his house, ready to sell. Boobie, Raye and Shaw committed an armed home invasion robbery and pistol whipped him until he revealed the location of the drugs. Cuban Shorty contacted Boobie and told him the drugs were his, but Boobie refused to return them. The following, day Michelle Feliciano and Cuban Shorty were driving by Bernard Shaw's house when they were shot at. Cuban Shorty returned fire, but from that day on, Cuban Shorty and Boobie hated each other.[9]

---

[9] Court testimony of Michelle Feliciano and an interview with

Willie "Too Sweet" Jones, who worked as a part time minister and a part time Sky Cap at the Ft. Lauderdale airport, was another source. The transactions with Too Sweet were usually conducted at the 79th Street Flea Market or his business, *Sweet's Auto World* in Miami that sold car and truck accessories such as rims, wheels, tires, car alarms and stereo systems.

Carlos Blanco furnished a sizable number of kilos of cocaine to Boobie. During the early 90s, Blanco obtained hundreds of kilos from a Colombian he knew only as "Francisco." Some of it, he learned, was smuggled into the United States from Colombia with the assistance of a pilot who flew for Avianca Airlines. The pilot would hide five kilos in the battery compartment of his plane on each flight he made to Miami. On one occasion, Boobie purchased a single kilo of heroin from Blanco for $75,000. Boobie told him that the "smack" was destined for Chicago.[10]

---

her conducted by Det. Joe Malott
[10]Court testimony of Carlos Blanco & interviews conducted by the author and DEA Agent Lenny Athas.

Literally, tons of cocaine were being spirited into South Florida through the Port of Miami on both cargo and passenger ships. This required the assistance of dock workers and others working at the Port to secretly offload it. The enticement of large sums of easy money caused many to risk losing their high paying union jobs, and even imprisonment.

No matter what method was used to smuggle the cocaine into Miami, though, there had to be a Colombian somewhere in the supply chain. Coca leaves are grown in Colombia, Bolivia, and Peru but 95% of the cocaine is processed in remote labs in the jungles of Colombia and controlled by the Colombian cartels.

So, in just two short years after being released from prison for murder, 20-year-old Kenneth "Boobie" Williams had successfully created an expansive narcotics network that operated in four states. But his greed and desire for more territory would soon result in a two-state gang war that caused the deaths of over a dozen people.

Figure 3. The Boobie Boys Gang.

Chapter 3
The Thomas Family

December 30, 1992

Jerrell Thomas couldn't believe his good luck.

While driving northbound on U.S. 441, he spotted Boobie at a gas station. Actually, he spotted Boobie's car first, a 1987 Blue Sterling. He and his crew had been searching for the Sterling and Boobie for weeks. (This is the same Sterling Gerry Dukes was driving when he was killed 15 months later). Thomas made a U-turn and parked on a residential street just north of the gas station. He pulled his .40 caliber Glock pistol from beneath the front seat of his pickup truck and grabbed an extra clip from the center console. He snuck through the yards to the rear of the station.

He saw Boobie with his back to him standing by the Sterling. Thomas was surprised to see him looking so fit. Just four months earlier, his brother Jerry had pumped five rounds into Boobie in the parking lot of the Club Rolexx strip club using the same Glock pistol he was now holding in his right hand. Jerry triumphantly told his brothers that he had killed Boobie and that they were rid of any threats from him forever. But Kenneth Williams survived, and Jerrell learned a few weeks ago that he had been released from the hospital. That's why the Thomas brothers and their gang were so frantically searching for him. They knew Boobie would be out for revenge and would not rest until he killed as many of them as he could.

He knew he couldn't mess up. But he did.

From sixty feet away, he emptied the 15-shot clip of his Glock at Boobie who immediately ducked upon hearing the gunshots. He inserted the second clip and emptied that, too. As he ran back to his vehicle panting, he was unsure if his bullets had found their mark. They did not. Boobie was left unscathed, but two innocent by-standers, who were near the gas pumps, were struck and killed by stray bullets.

Magnus Hamilton, a 45-year-old accountant from Perrine, Florida was struck in the head. The projectile entered his left eye, traversed his brain, and exited through the back of his skull. He was dead on the scene. He was survived by his wife and two children.

Everold Johnson, a 36-year-old tourist from Queens, New York, was hit twice in the back. Both bullets exited his chest. He was rushed to a nearby hospital but expired in the emergency room. Johnson was in town to visit his fiancée and had stopped at the gas station to buy lottery tickets.

Jerrell Thomas was captured by uniform police officers while fleeing in his burgundy pick-up truck and charged with the two murders.

Jerrell Thomas, along with his brothers, Virgil, Jerry, and Aaron, were small-time drug dealers in North Miami-Dade County until they struck it rich in Virginia. They were introduced by a mutual friend to Keith "Fat Keith" Williams (no relation to Kenneth Williams). Fat Keith controlled the dispersal of drugs in the government housing projects in Norfolk and Portsmouth.

Fat Keith told them that he was willing to buy as much cocaine as they could bring him. The brothers started out slowly by transporting ounces, but because they were making so much money so fast, they were soon up to three kilos every two weeks. They purchased the cocaine from "Too Sweet Willie" at his rim shop in Miami for $18,000 per kilo and sold it to Fat Keith for $30,000.

Things were running smoothly until an unexpected event changed everything. Fat Keith's girlfriend "Poochie" shot and killed him in a domestic quarrel. Poochie's real name was Andra Brownlee, and she was originally from Miami. Rumors spread that she was having a sexual relationship with Aaron Thomas and that she did not kill Fat Keith in self-defense, but intentionally.[11]

Nevertheless, with Fat Keith dead, there was a void that the Thomas Family stepped into and filled. The Thomas Family was now in control of all the cocaine and crack sales in the lucrative markets of Norfolk and Portsmouth. In order to protect their newly acquired territory, the Thomases imported "enforcers" from Miami. Business was soon booming.

The Thomases continued purchasing from Too Sweet Willie, but because of the increase in demand, they eventually forged a deal with Carlos Diaz to buy ten kilos every five days at a discounted price of $15,500 each.

The money was rolling in. Too much money as it turned out. When Too Sweet Willie's rim shop was shut down by the Feds for money laundering, the Thomases bought his entire inventory and set up their own store called *Ground Effects International* in Virginia Beach. It was a front to launder money.

---

[11] From the court testimony of Sadat Muhammed, who was Fat Keith's cousin. And from interviews with Muhammed conducted by the author and Detective Jeff Lewis.

March/April 1992

Word got back to Carol City that the Thomases had Virginia "locked down" and were making massive amounts of money. Boobie took his longtime friend, Darryl Green, and Green's father-in-law, Phillip Williams, with him to Norfolk to challenge the Thomas' operation.

Initially, they began by selling drugs in the oceanfront area away from the Thomas' domain, but after about a month, they directly provoked the Thomases by selling on their turf. The Thomas brothers confronted them with guns and told them to "get out and stay out." That same night, Williams and Green returned to the projects and shot multiple rounds into a crowd, wounding several people. No one was killed, but the message was clear.

The next night, Green's unoccupied truck was shot full of holes. Two nights later, a drive-by shooting occurred at the Thomas family compound in North Miami-Dade County.

Jerrell Thomas was with Bennie Brownlee three weeks later when they encountered Boobie, Darryl Green, and Michael "Chico" Harper at a Flea Market in Carol City.

Boobie told Thomas, "Y'all are going to have to share all that money you makin' or there's going to be a war."

Jerrell was unimpressed. "Whatever. I ain't sharing my shit, so you better bring it on, because I don't owe you nothin'," he said.[12]

Less than a week later, Lawrence Brown, who worked for the Thomases, was at a stoplight in Norfolk when two gunmen with hoods over their faces shot him five times. Transported to Sentara Hospital in critical condition, he was confined to the intensive care unit for three weeks and eventually recovered. The war had started, and it would continue for the next two years, causing untold casualties on both sides.

---

[12] From an interview with Jerrell Thomas by the author.

Jason Ortega was there for all of it. Ortega first met Boobie in the early 90s through his father, Diego DeJesus, whom he described as a "major doper." Ortega committed numerous "rip offs" of dope dealers with Boobie and Darryl Green when they first started out. It was the money and narcotics Boobie received from these robberies that propelled him so quickly into a major player in the narcotics business. For his part, Ortega never shared in the "take," which many times amounted to multiple kilos of cocaine and hundreds of thousands of dollars. He was paid a flat fee of $2,000 per robbery and was content with that.[13]

Using the proceeds from the drug rips, Boobie started out modestly because he and Green only knew how to cook one ounce of crack at a time. This slowed down their distribution capabilities considerably. Eventually, they were able to increase their output, and the business expanded rapidly. Boobie opened a second operation in

---

[13] Numerous interviews are conducted with Ortega by the author and Det. Jeff Lewis.

Pensacola, a third in Tallahassee, and a fourth in Jacksonville run by Arthur Lee, who was from the Matchboxes. Boobie often complained to Ortega that Arthur Lee was not moving enough product but that he was reluctant to replace him because he was so close to Lee's mother, Angel. Boobie even referred to her as his Godmother.

Arthur Lee was eventually arrested by the DEA for conspiracy to traffic cocaine and Heroin. The case against him was airtight. His fingerprints were found throughout a stash house on packages of heroin and cocaine and on the beakers used to cook the crack.

Because these locations became so profitable so quickly, Boobie was able to open another "drug hole" in Raleigh, North Carolina, which was supervised by Darryl Green.

Boobie then set his sights on Norfolk, Virginia. He was shocked by the resistance that was mounted by the Thomas brothers. In every other acquisition he had made, he would simply show up with five or six "shooters" armed with AK-47s, who would riddle the cars of the local dealers with bullet holes and announce, "the Miami Boys are here." This would always result in a swift and orderly transfer of control. But the Thomases were different. They refused to relinquish their turf without a fight.

One person saw Boobie's incursion as an opportunity. That person was Richard Stitt, whose nickname was "Death."[14] He ran a small narcotics operation in the Oceanview section apart from the Thomas Family, and he was ambitious. He realized that by aligning himself with Boobie, together they could supplant the Thomases. Within weeks of joining forces with the "Miami Boys," Stitt and Boobie were in control of the Sweetbriar and Brittany housing projects. The income produced by these new operations enabled Boobie to expand his network to Hartford, Connecticut and Pittsburgh, Pennsylvania. He formed an alliance with two drug dealers from Hampton, Virginia to open the Pittsburgh

---

[14] Stitt's close friend, Brain Mackey went by the nickname, "Destruction." Together they were known as "Death and Destruction."

enterprise. He sent Darrell Ward (aka: "Slinky") from the Matchboxes to oversee Pittsburgh. Within a few months, Slinky's decomposed body was found in the trunk of a car. He had been shot once in the back of the head. The medical examiner estimated he had been in the trunk for at least two weeks. Undeterred, Boobie put Slinky's wife, Anna Ward, in charge. Ward was originally from England.[15]

Because Stitt was not opposed to using violence, he moved up quicky in the chain of command. When Jason Ortega arrived back in Virginia in 1992, he found himself under Stitt in the hierarchy of the organization. This was fine with Ortega. He viewed himself as a well-paid "soldier" and wanted nothing to do with the pressures of command. He was satisfied with his station in the group. He liked being paid for the tasks he performed and not being burdened by "making decisions or keeping the money straight." He described Boobie as a "good boss."

---

[15] From an interview with Pittsburgh homicide Sgt. Paul Marraway conducted by the author.

As the war raged on, Ortega and Stitt engaged in multiple shootouts with the Thomas Gang. Ortega also noticed that more and more enforcers he knew from the Matchboxes were showing up in Virginia to augment Boobie's forces. The most vicious of these were Linard Albury (aka: Shotout) and Shawntelle Seay (aka: Red Boy), who had reputations as "stone killers."

Ortega was given the task of acquiring firearms for the Boobie Boys. Initially, Boobie purchased all the AK-47s he needed from a Russian who owned a strip club in Orlando, but they had a falling out, and Ortega was named the armorer for the group. He combed the want ads of newspapers in Virginia and Miami. He attended gun shows and visited dozens of pawn shops. He became so adept at locating weapons that there was always an ample supply.

During interviews, Ortega revealed many interesting tidbits about Boobie. For instance, Boobie had a penchant for burying his money, "like a pirate." He would routinely stuff tens of thousands of dollars into waterproof Tupperware containers and secretly bury them. Cemeteries, open fields, and canal banks were his favorite locations to hide the money.

And, just like a pirate, he would make a map denoting the exact location of the "treasure." Ortega recalled one instance when Boobie buried $60,000 in Pensacola, and even with the aid of a map, was unable to locate it. He and Boobie spent an entire day searching and eventually found it. Occasionally, he would bury kilos of cocaine in the same manner.

Boobie was enamored with "big names" such as Tupac Shakur, Mike Tyson, and other personalities. He would visit Las Vegas often to attend concerts and prize fights. He knew Tupac and Tyson personally and had numerous photographs taken with them. Ortega accompanied Boobie on many of these trips to Las Vegas. He was with Boobie in Vegas the night Tupac was murdered. The next day, Boobie had a picture of him with Tupac silk screened onto dozens of T-shirts that he handed out to his friends and associates.[16]

Boobie was also a heavy gambler. Ortega once witnessed him betting $10,000, with another dope dealer, on a single game of pool.

Both Stitt and Ortega committed multiple murders for Boobie. On one occasion, Ortega was ordered by Stitt to kill James Gilliam, Jr. It was suspected that Gilliam had stolen narcotics from a Miami shipment. Ortega stalked Gilliam at his home and walked up to him as he stepped out of his vehicle. He pointed a .38 caliber revolver at his head and shouted, "Freeze." Gilliam recognized Ortega immediately and said, "Stop playing, Jason." Ortega then shot him twice in the face. Gilliam collapsed and died instantly in his driveway. Gilliam's roommate, Alton Lopez, was also killed. He was shot in the

---

[16] When arrested, Ortega still had one of the shirts. It was seized by the Virginia Beach Police Department along with numerous handguns and three AK-47s.

back of the head while talking on a pay phone at a nearby convenience store. Ortega participated in a third murder ordered by Stitt in which Sinclair Simon was shot and killed.

(Ortega was eventually charged with multiple murders. He pleaded guilty and agreed to testify against Stitt. Because of his cooperation, the Feds waived the death penalty, and he was sentenced to life in prison plus 30 years. Further cooperation resulted in his release in 2020).

As teenagers, Boobie and the Thomas brothers were actually friends, but now the greed for power and money undermined all previous relationships. The violence that raged in Virginia would soon make its way back to the streets of Miami.

CHAPTER 4
Bennie Brownlee

March 17, 1994
10:30 p.m.

Bennie Brownlee, and Marlon Randall just killed Boobie. Or so they thought.

Two hours earlier, they, along with Walter Betterson (aka: Fatso) and Derrick Young (aka: Hollywood), spotted Boobie's blue Sterling parked along the side of Zeus's barber shop. They hurriedly retrieved two AK-47s, a .223 rifle, and a shotgun from a girlfriend's apartment. The four of them then parked across the street from the barber shop and waited.

Boobie had given Gerry Dukes his car several weeks earlier and told him to be careful. He said the Sterling was "hot" because the Thomas Family knew that he always drove it. Dukes didn't seem concerned even though he did somewhat resemble Boobie.

When Dukes emerged from the barber

shop and was unlocking the Sterling, the four members of the Thomas Gang: Brownlee, Randall, Betterson, and Young, opened up on him with their weapons. As they ran back to their getaway car, they were jubilant. They repeatedly high-fived each other, believing they had just murdered Boobie.

Within twenty minutes, Dan Johnson received a telephone call from Fatso and Hollywood who excitedly told him that they had just killed Boobie at Zeus's barber shop. Johnson frowned when he heard the news. He was friends with both Fatso and Boobie and had been trying to mediate the tensions between them. He drove to Fatso's house where they told him how they shot Boobie over and over and there was no chance that he survived. They showed him the AK-47s and the .223 rifle that were used in the attack.

Johnson left Fatso's house and drove his green Duly pick-up truck to the Carol City shopping center where he learned that it was not Boobie who had been killed, but

Gerry Dukes. He called Fatso and Hollywood and informed them that they had killed the wrong person. They were horrified.

Johnson met with Boobie and told him that the killing of Dukes was a mistake. Boobie was not sympathetic. He told Johnson to let Fatso and Hollywood know that "they were dead men."

March 18,1994
1 a.m.

The word quickly spread that Boobie was still alive. Bennie Brownlee and Marlon Randle knew that Boobie would now hunt them down. They decided to hide out at Marlon's sister, Zandra's, apartment on NW 37th Avenue. Brownlee pulled his tan Honda Accord into the east parking lot of the complex, and just as he exited the car, he spotted two armed men with hoods and masks covering their faces jogging toward him. He tried to run but both men opened fire and cut him down with AK-47s. Two security guards witnessed the entire incident. The autopsy revealed that the muscular 19-year-old victim had twenty-three entrance and exit wounds to his body. Both lungs had collapsed because of the multiple gunshot wounds to his chest. His left kidney and liver were shredded. His spinal cord was severed by at least one of the bullets.

Marlon Randle was able to escape by crouching between two parked cars. The shooters never knew he was there. Because of the dark tinted windows on the Accord, they were unaware that he was a passenger. He escaped unharmed but returned to the scene to identify Brownlee's body for Fire Rescue personnel.

Homicide Sergeant Felix Jimenez and his squad, who were on-call, responded to the parking lot and assumed responsibility for the murder investigation. While scouring the crime scene for clues, they were able to locate a beeper that was apparently dropped by one of the shooters as he fled though the courtyard of the complex. Lead detective, Gus Bayas, called the

Communications Bureau Shift Commander and obtained an emergency contact number for the owner of the beeper store that issued it. He quickly learned that the beeper was leased to Marvin Rogers, a close associate of Boobie.

Figure 4. Bennie Brownlee. Killed in retaliation for the murder of Gerry Dukes. (Miami-Dade County Clerk of the Court)

The next day, a large contingent of the Boobie Boys showed up at Jackson Memorial Hospital and surrounded Johnnie Hankins bed. They told him in graphic detail how they had killed one of his and Gerry Dukes's assailants. The group included Boobie, Marvin Rogers, Chico (Michael Harper), Bernard Shaw,

Ronald Raye, and Fish Grease (Corey Mucherson).

Marvin Rogers and Boobie admitted to being the shooters and Chico said he drove the getaway car. The others acknowledged that they were also present but did not elaborate on their roles.

Marvin Rogers gleefully described how he shot Brownlee over and over as he was sprawled on the ground and how he "bounced up and down." He also expressed his concern over losing his beeper as he fled. He was worried that the police would find his fingerprints on it.

Hankins was still in critical condition and suffering from multiple wounds. The group became so loud recounting the shooting and laughing about how Brownlee died "with a scared look on his face," that the nursing staff insisted that they leave. Before leaving, Boobie told Hankins that he knew who the other shooters were that attacked him and Dukes and that he was going to "take care of it."[17]

---

[17] From court testimony and an interview conducted with

March 20, 1994
3 a.m.

Aaron Thomas and Wayne Brownlee had been playing Nintendo at Richard James's house into the wee hours of the morning. As they were driving home, they noticed a dark green Volvo following them. When they turned a corner, the streetlights illuminated the inside of the Volvo. They were able to see Boobie in the front passenger seat and Mike "Chico" Harper behind the wheel. Boobie leaned his upper body out of the passenger window and sprayed their vehicle with an AK-47. They heard loud "thumps" and "pings" as multiple projectiles struck the metal trunk and side of their car. All the windows were blown out in seconds. Aaron Thomas was driving and attempted to flee into a residential neighborhood, but the green Volvo continued to chase them, with Boobie shooting wildly. The pursuit was finally halted when they saw a Metro police car parked at a gas station and screamed for help. Boobie and Chico slipped away into the darkness. Wayne Brownlee was struck by multiple bullets and hospitalized. Aaron Thomas was cut by the shattered glass but otherwise unharmed.[18]

Wayne Brownlee was Bennie Brownlee's cousin and the brother of Ricky Brownlee. On the night Wayne was shot, Ricky was in a halfway house near Opa-Locka airport after having served time in prison for the sale of cocaine. Although in 1994 Ricky was considered a minor player in the dope business, in just five years, he would become the biggest and most feared narcotics kingpin in Miami-Dade County. Even bigger than Boobie.

Ricky Brownlee would eventually control a nine-block area in the city of Opa-Locka known as "the Triangle," and he would be dubbed "the unofficial Mayor of Opa-Locka" due to the power he exerted. When he was firmly established, he was moving over 100 kilos of powdered cocaine *per week*.

---

[18] From an interview with Aaron Thomas by Det. Jeff Lewis.

His rise to infamy paralleled Boobie's, even though he was 15 years older. Born in 1956, he was one of ten children. He grew up poor, wearing hand me downs and sleeping with seven of his siblings in the same room. Ricky was a born entrepreneur. He set up Kool-Aid and popsicle stands in the neighborhood as a youngster. He cut lawns, and at the age of twelve had a paper route. At Carol City High School, he was a standout athlete, competing in football, basketball, and swimming. During his senior year, just before graduation, he abruptly joined the army. He was honorably discharged two years later and returned to Opa-Locka.

For the next several years, Ricky Brownlee was in and out of jail on narcotics and firearms charges. Then, in 1983, he was arrested for selling a kilo of cocaine to an undercover DEA agent. He was locked up for nearly 10 years but used Atlanta Federal prison as an institution of higher learning. He soaked up as much information about the narcotics business as he could. He listened raptly to story after story told by drug traffickers as they described how they were caught and the mistakes they made.

When he was released, he used this accumulated knowledge to build his own empire. His big break came when the largest cocaine trafficker in Miami-Dade County, Isaac Hicks, was arrested, convicted, and sentenced to life in Federal Prison. This created a void that Brownlee eagerly filled. Both Ricky Brownlee and Boobie rose to power at the same time in the 90s but were careful to avoid conflict with each other over turf, knowing that an internecine war would be bloody and counterproductive.

Brownlee is credited with creating the 8 Ball. An 8 Ball is one eighth of an ounce or 3.5 grams of cocaine. Street lore says that Ricky wanted an amount smaller than a kilo, half kilo, or even a quarter kilo, that he could sell at a price street level buyers could afford. He started by selling 8 Balls for $50.00 each. Several buyers often pooled their money to make the purchase.

The name Brownlee was well known to

homicide detectives in Miami-Dade County. The *Miami Herald* once reported that an audit conducted by the Medical Examiner's Office determined that in the 80s and 90s, Brownlee was the most murdered surname in the county. More so than even the names Hernandez and Gonzalez.

Paradoxically, Ricky Brownlee used both fear and good will to maintain control. Anyone crossing him was inevitably found dead. Those murders were rarely solved.

But he was also a community benefactor. He bought equipment and uniforms for the local youth football, basketball, and baseball teams. He handed out free turkeys at Thanksgiving and Christmas. He paid the funeral bills for the families who couldn't afford them. He paid the light bills of the poor when their power was turned off. He was known to hand out $50 bills to the homeless. All this charity bought loyalty and silence when the police started asking questions. This is a strategy he learned from a predecessor in the narcotics business named Bunky Brown. Brown was the first benevolent doper in Miami-Dade County. Others followed his lead, including Boobie. They all realized that it is always better to have the community beholden to you rather than snitching against you. Over the years, this "Robin Hood" ploy has been used effectively by drug lords in big cities and small towns all over the country.

Figure 5. Drug Kingpin Ricky Brownlee. (Mobb Ties)

March 26, 1994
2 p.m.

Gerry Dukes's funeral service was held

at the Christian Fellowship Missionary Baptist Church in Miami. The family first learned of Gerry's death from Boobie when he came to the house crying on the night of the murder. Between sobs, he told Gerry's brother, Vincent, "I'm going to take care of it." He left quickly saying, "I'm going to go recruit some people and get them back for killing Gerry." The next day, Boobie showed up at the house again, still crying, and handed a piece of paper with names on it to Gerry's mother. He told her that the people named on the list would be the pallbearers.[19]

The funeral procession traveled from the church to Dade Memorial Park on Opa-Locka Boulevard. Gerry Dukes's sister, Tangela, and the rest of the family rode with Boobie in a Cadillac provided by the Range Funeral Home.[20] Tangela had

---

[19] From an interview with Vincent Dukes conducted by the author.

[20] Range Funeral Home is owned by Athalie Range, a community activist. In 1965 she was the first Black woman elected to the Miami City Commission. In 1970 she was appointed as Secretary of the Department of Community Affairs making her the first African American to serve as head of a Florida state agency since reconstruction. She has been

known Boobie since the second grade. While she was standing next to Boobie at the gravesite, he gently nudged her and pointed with his chin to the other side of the cemetery where a family was huddled under a green tent, surrounding a fresh grave.

"That's the fuck nigger that killed your brother, right there," Boobie said. "That's his family. He got what he deserved."[21]

Later that day, Tangela was told by friends that the grave Boobie pointed to was that of Bennie Brownlee who was killed three hours after her brother.[22]

---

inducted into the Florida Womens Hall of Fame. She died in 2006 at the age of 91.

[21] Court testimony of Charles Young and from an interview conducted by the author.

[22] From an interview conducted with Tangela Dukes by Det. Chuck Clark and the author.

CHAPTER 5
Walter Betterson and Derek Young

Fatso and Hollywood had been looking over their shoulders for the past three months. They knew Boobie was trying to kill them. He wanted revenge for the death of his friend Gerry Dukes. They also knew that the only thing that could save them was if they were able to kill Boobie first. It's not like they hadn't been trying, but Boobie was just as wary as they were.

Fatso confided to his mother and sister that someone was trying to kill him. He told them that Boobie thought he "set up" Gerry Dukes to be killed. He didn't tell them that he was, in fact, one of the killers. He tempered his narrative by claiming he was only peripherally involved. Fatso's mother, Cleoa Betterson, offered to talk to Boobie and "straighten things out" on her son's behalf.

Fatso gave her a wry smile. "It doesn't work that way, Ma," he said sadly and stared off into the distance.[23]

Unlike Fatso, Hollywood told his father, Charles Young, the whole truth regarding Dukes's murder. Within hours after Dukes's death, Hollywood informed his father that he, Fatso, Bennie Brownlee, and Marlon Randall killed Dukes at Zeus's barber shop.[24] Charles Young was unfazed. He was a career criminal who had been in and out of prison his whole life. When Derek and his younger brother, Maurice, were barely teenagers, their father had them selling cocaine in the Liberty Square housing projects in the heart of Liberty City.

Built in 1937 during the Roosevelt Administration, Liberty Square contained 735 units. Heralded as the first public housing projects in the Southern United States, they were nicknamed the "Pork and Beans" because of the orange doors on every apartment. They evolved into one of the most violent, crime-ridden housing projects in all Miami-Dade County.

---

[23] From an interview with Cleoa Betterson conducted by Det. Chuck Clark.

[24] Court testimony of Charles Young and from an interview conducted by the author.

As juveniles, both Hollywood and his brother were arrested numerous times for the sale of cocaine, but because they were not yet adults, they were quickly released back into their father's custody. Hollywood's brother, Maurice, at the age of fifteen, was arrested on a charge of attempted murder for nearly killing another teenager in a shoot-out over drugs. He was convicted as an adult and sentenced as a youthful offender, just like Boobie.

Upon his release from prison, Maurice Young, using the name Trick Daddy began rapping locally. Producer Ted Lucas of *Slip and Slide Records* saw his potential and signed him to a record contract. His big break came when he was featured on an album released by Luther Campbell and *2Live Crew*.

From 1998 to 2009, Trick Daddy had seven albums that reached the top 10 on Billboard's Top Rap and R&B charts. His hit single, *I'm a Thug* reached number seven on Billboard's Hot 100. His music was featured on the soundtracks of several hit movies including *Training Day* starring Denzel Washington, *Exit Wounds* starring Steven Segal and *The A-Team* with Bradley Cooper.

Trick Daddy beat the odds and escaped from the Pork and Beans. He achieved international fame and acquired fabulous wealth, but he still embraced the gangster lifestyle for most of his career. He was arrested several times for narcotics and firearms violations, and he always surrounded himself with a posse of cutthroats and criminals.

One of Trick Daddy's biggest hits, *Shut Up*, was recorded with Katrina Taylor who was known musically as "Trina." Trina was his brother Hollywood's girlfriend and had grown up in Liberty City with Hollywood and Trick Daddy. She was a drum majorette at Miami Northwestern High School, and after graduation, she started studying to acquire her real estate license. She wrote rap lyrics in her spare time. One night, Trick Daddy heard her do an impromptu rap at a party and asked her to appear on a track called *Nann Nigga*, for his upcoming album. The track was released as a single and became a regional hit, reaching number 62 on Billboard's Hot 100. Following the success of *Nann Nigga*, Trina gave up her real estate career and began rapping professionally. She became known for her sexually charged and profane lyrics.

Trina's career in the music industry spanned 20 years and included six studio albums, 10 BET Award nominations, two ASCAP Awards, two BMI Awards, one Billboard Music Award, one EME Award, and one All Star Music Award. She was described as "the most consistent female rapper of all time" in 2012 by XXL and was honored by Billboard as one of the "31 Female Rappers Who Changed Hip-Hop" in 2014.

All of this would occur in the future. At the time of the Boobie Boys/Thomas Family feud, Trina was simply Katrina Taylor, Hollywood's girlfriend.

June 22, 1994
1 p.m.

Charles Young helped Fatso and Hollywood transfer ten kilos of cocaine from his van into their vehicle. He instructed them to deliver it to a Latin male in Opa-Locka. He watched them as they packed it in the trunk of a 1987 Buick Grand National. The drugs were hidden in the spare tire compartment beneath some tires, newspapers, and clothing. Young lived near the Miami Dolphins' football stadium, and it was a short drive down 27th Avenue to Opa-Locka. He told them to drive cautiously and to not attract the attention of the police.

Less than an hour later, Hollywood called his father to say they had stopped by Fatso's house to pick up some music CDs but were on their way to deliver the cocaine. They left the house and drove eastbound on NW 152nd Street.

Twenty-seven-year-old Johnnie Hampton was sitting on the front porch of his mother's residence holding his 10-month-old son, Johnnie Junior, when he heard gunfire. He brought the baby inside and handed him to his mother. As he walked back outside, he saw a black Buick Grand National being chased by two other vehicles, a black Impala and powder blue Oldsmobile. The passengers in the pursuing vehicles were leaning out of the windows shooting at the Buick.

The sidewalks in Hampton's neighborhood were being repaired, and the Buick hit some of the construction equipment. It spun out striking several parked cars and ended up wedged between a mound of dirt and a pickup truck. The two vehicles blocked the Buick in as four gunmen emerged and began firing into it. Fatso and Hollywood tried to escape, but they were trapped. Hampton recognized Boobie and one of the Twins, Leonard "Bo" Brown, as two of the shooters. The other two shooters had their faces covered with masks. Boobie was dressed head to toe in camouflage clothing. Bo had on all black and was armed with a chrome-plated automatic pistol. Boobie and one of the masked gunmen had AK-47s which they used to unleash a barrage of gunfire, poking both barrels into the broken windows of the Buick as they fired. Fatso and Hollywood didn't have a chance. They were slaughtered.

Hampton crouched behind a parked car to protect himself and watched the entire incident as it unfolded. The shooting occurred directly in front of his mother's house, and he was only several feet away. He was close enough to hear a conversation between Boobie and Bo after the shooting had stopped and gun smoke still hung in the air.

"I guess those fuck niggers ain't so tough now," Boobie said.

"They ain't shit. Fuck 'em," Bo replied.

After the Boobie Boys fled in their vehicles, Hampton, and several of his neighbors, who had also witnessed the attack, ventured into the street, and peered into the Grand National. They were sickened by what they saw. Fatso and Hollywood's bodies were mutilated by dozens of .762mm rounds. Hampton, who lived only doors away from Fatso and had known him his whole life, didn't even realize it was him. His head had been blown apart and his brain was exposed. His face was unrecognizable.

The next day, Hampton was again sitting on his mother's front porch when the same black Impala that was involved in the shooting drove by very slowly. Because of the dark tinted windows, he was unable to see the occupants but was so unnerved that he insisted that his mother move from the house for her own safety. He moved her that afternoon. He now knew firsthand how dangerous the Boobie Boys could be.[25]

Figure 6. The bodies of Fatso and Hollywood were so badly mangled that the car was towed to the Medical Examiner's Office where they were removed. (Miami-Dade County Clerk

[25] From Court testimony of Johnnie Hampton and an interview conducted by the author.

of the Court)

It was nearly 4 a.m. The sun wouldn't rise for another three hours. My team along with three other homicide teams were staged with 10 DEA agents in the east parking lot of Joe Robbie Stadium, where the Miami Dolphins played their home games.

Today would be the end of the Thomas Family drug organization. A two-year DEA investigation had culminated in the issuance of fifteen arrest warrants and eight search warrants in both Miami and Virginia. Two SWAT teams were part of our entourage and would conduct any high-risk entries. There were six locations that we intended to hit simultaneously at daybreak. Four were in North Miami-Dade County. These were the residences of the Thomas brothers and their parents. One in Broward County was the apartment of one of Aaron Thomas's girlfriends, and the sixth was the home of Richard James, a lieutenant for the Thomases.

On my way to the staging area, I

conducted a drive-by of the Thomas brothers' homes in a non-descript rental car. All three had swimming pools in the backyards, and bars on the windows. The front and back doors were also heavily barred. Aaron Thomas's house had two huge Rottweilers patrolling inside of a wrought iron fence.

When I described the houses to SWAT Lieutenant Tom Futch, he decided he wanted to look for himself. I drove him by the houses, and when we returned to the staging area, he ordered two county wreckers to be used to pull off two of the front doors. The SWAT truck would be used on the third door.

We divided up into teams that contained three homicide detectives and at least one DEA agent. The teams took up positions near each of the six target locations. At 6:50 a.m., Detective Steve Parr notified everyone on the police radio that Judge Leonard Glick had just signed the search warrants, and we all moved in.

The synchronized raids went off without a hitch. I was assigned to Aaron Thomas's location. I watched as one of the SWAT team members snuck up to the metal front door and attached a cable from the wrecker to the bars. When the wrecker driver hit the gas, the door flew off its hinges, tumbling in the air end over end until it finally came to rest on the front lawn. As planned, everyone inside was still asleep. Within minutes, Aaron Thomas was in handcuffs, and the house was secure. We later learned that the raids in Virginia had gone just as smoothly.

The arrests in Miami and Virginia completely dismantled the Thomas organization. The case put together by the DEA's office in Virginia was so solid that nearly all of the defendants elected to plead guilty. The sentences they received were hefty. Many of us in the Homicide Bureau believed that this would end the carnage. With most of the Thomas Family in Federal prison, we assumed the killings would finally stop. We were wrong.

Part Two

CHAPTER 6
Roger Davis and Tyrone Tarver

February 11, 1998
6 p.m.

I scanned the parking lot of the Amoco gas station on NW 62nd Street and saw shell casings scattered on the pavement between the gas pumps. A crime lab technician was placing sequentially numbered placards near each casing, and she was already up to forty-three.

A Northside District uniform officer wrote down my name as I ducked under the crime scene tape.

"It looks like a massacre," I said.

"It is," he said grimly. "You have two victims, Sarge. Detective Lewis is already here."

I walked to the rear of the station where I saw one of the victims lying near a dumpster. His body had been riddled with bullets. He was face up, his eyes were open, and his long dread locks were splayed out in a large pool of bright red blood. Small rivulets of blood that had drained out of his body were slowly making their way down the sloped driveway. Detective Jeff Lewis was standing near the dead man's feet rapidly jotting down notes on a yellow legal pad. He glanced up at me as I approached.

"We've got a second victim who was transported to JMH. He's in bad shape, probably won't make it. He was hit multiple times, too. According to witnesses, there were two shooters who got out of a green Altima and just opened up on them," he said.

The dead man lying near the dumpster was 27-year-old, Roger Davis, the father of five children. He had pulled into the station earlier to fill up his 1967 Chevrolet Caprice with gas. He was on his way home from an appointment at a local veterinarian. His dog, Yayo, was in the car with him. (Yayo is street slang for cocaine). As he stopped near the outside pumps, he smiled when he saw another 1967 Chevrolet Caprice already parked there.

His Caprice was light green and the other Caprice, that he knew belonged to Tyrone Tarver, was black. Both were in mint condition. Davis and Tarver knew each other casually from the neighborhood and were both proud of their "rides." They stood between the pumps slapping each other's hands in a "homie handshake," and smiling broadly as they complimented one another on how immaculate their respective cars looked. They didn't notice the dark green Nissan that drove into the *Amoco* behind them.

Two masked gunmen sprang from the vehicle and began firing at Davis and Tarver. They were armed with AK-47s. Tyrone Tarver fled toward 22nd avenue, and Roger Davis fled to the rear of the gas station. One of the AK-47 shooters fired multiple rounds into Tarver, and he collapsed in the street. He writhed in pain on the pavement screaming, "It burns! It burns!" And then he lost consciousness.

The other assassin chased Davis to the rear of the station where he was trapped near a dumpster. He got down on his knees, threw up his hands, and begged for his life.

"Please don't," he cried.

Unmoved, the gunman fired several rounds directly into his chest from six feet away. When he fell on his back, the shooter calmly stepped forward, pressed the muzzle to his forehead and shot him again. Both assailants reentered the green vehicle and fled.

Two women who lived on 61st Street directly behind the Poitier Funeral home were sitting on their front porch when they heard the volley of gunfire at the *Amoco*. Moments later, they watched as a dark green Nissan Altima barreled down their street and skidded to a stop behind a white Toyota Camry. Four men dressed in camouflage hurriedly exited the Altima, got into the Camry, and sped off. One of the women memorized the tag number on the Camry as it drove away. She flagged down two police cars who were searching in the area and gave the information to the officers.

Detective Mike Hernandez responded to

the hospital to interview the second victim, Tyrone Tarver, but when he inquired about him in the emergency room, he was told that he had died in the Fire Rescue truck on the way there. Mike made arrangements for the body to be transported to the ME's Office for an autopsy.

Using his hand-held radio, Jeff ran two license tags on "channel D" (the records frequency). The first was the tag number on the green Altima. Uniformed officers had secured that vehicle as a secondary crime scene. The channel D dispatcher quickly informed him that the Nissan Altima was reported stolen. No big surprise. We couldn't be so lucky as to have the killers in a double murder use a car registered to themselves. It had been stolen over a month ago from the parking lot of the *El Dorado* furniture store in Carol City.

The second license plate he ran was on the white Camry. (The one that the woman sitting on her front porch had committed to memory). That tag was registered to a rental vehicle. Jeff issued a countywide BOLO (Be On the Look Out), hoping to locate it occupied.

When the crime lab finished at the *Amoco* gas station, they made their way to where the Altima had been abandoned. They impounded two AK-47s and four identical black ski masks from the interior of the vehicle. One of the AK-47 rifles was an Egyptian military Maadi and the other a Chinese Norinco. The Norinco is a "knock off" of the original Russian rifle. The Egyptian model is very similar to the actual Russian prototype.

Norinco is the government owned weapons supplier of the Communist Chinese Party (CCP). Like many products the Chinese manufacture, the Norinco AK is a stolen design. They took actual Russian AK-47s that were captured in Vietnam, reverse-engineered how they were constructed, and created the Type-56. This weapon eventually morphed into the MAK 90, (production of the weapon started in 1990 therefore MAK 90 stands for Model AK 1990). The MAK 90 was produced only in a semi-automatic version so that it could be imported and sold in the lucrative gun markets in the United States. Because they are light and compact, they were also mass produced for the tank crews in the Chinese Army.

In the 1950s, as part of a Soviet Union military aid program initiated in the Republic of Egypt, a factory was opened in the city of Maadi, where the AK-47 was manufactured by Egyptian workers who were trained and supervised by Russians. In 1982, Anwar Sadat expelled the Russians from Egypt, but by then, the fabrication of the rifles was fully established, and production continued. Tens of thousands of both the Norinco MAC 90 and the Egyptian Maadi rifles have been imported into the United States.

Figure 7. Roger Davis, 27, was executed at the Amoco gas station. (Miami-Dade Clerk of the Court).

At 4 a.m., Jeff was awakened by his pager. He had been asleep less than three hours. He called the Homicide Office, and the midnight detective told him that the Toyota Camry he had broadcast a BOLO on had been located. It was spotted by a passing motorist in an open field near County Line Road, fully engulfed in flames. Firefighters extinguished the fire and quickly determined that it was arson. Gasoline had been poured into the interior of the vehicle, and it had been set ablaze.

Detectives Jeff Lewis and Mike

Hernandez were waiting at the front door of the *Enterprise* car rental facility near the airport when the manager arrived to open at 7 a.m. She located the rental agreement for the Camry and gave it to the detectives. It had been leased to one, Tanaka Stringer, who, interestingly enough, lived two blocks from where the car had been incinerated. A second driver was listed on the paperwork as Errol Joseph, with the same address.

When Jeff and Mike knocked on Tanaka Stringer's door, she was less than cooperative. She claimed that she had no idea where the Camry was. She said that the last time she saw it, Errol, who "she didn't know very well" was driving it. When they told her it had been seen fleeing from a double murder, she just shrugged and said, "That ain't none of me." No amount of threatening or cajoling could convince her to tell them more.

On the way back to the Homicide Office, Jeff stopped and spoke with the owner of the stolen Altima. She said that her cell phone was in the car when it was taken.

When she received her monthly cell phone bill, there were numerous numbers that she didn't recognize. A total of 110 calls to be exact. These calls were made after the car and phone had been stolen. She gave the itemized section of the bill that listed the numbers to Jeff. He immediately recognized that one of the numbers belonged to Tanaka Stringer. She had provided it to him less than an hour earlier when he interviewed her and asked her for contact information.

Back at the office, he began cold calling several of the numbers. A phone number frequently called in Titusville, Florida was answered by a woman who identified herself as Eleanor Horne. When she was asked who had called her repeatedly from a Carol City cell phone number, she said the caller was her boyfriend, Cory Mucherson, who was also known as Fish Grease.[26]

---

[26] From court testimony and an interview with Det. Joe Malott.

This was the same Corey Mucherson who was a known member of the Boobie Boys during the Gerry Dukes murder investigation back in 1994. There were more revelations to come.

February 13, 1998
3 a.m.

Georgia Highway Patrol (GHP) Trooper William Taylor drove his blue and orange marked vehicle across the grassy median that separated the north and southbound lanes of Interstate 75. Trooper Taylor was part of a drug interdiction unit. He and his canine partner, Dooley, a Belgian Malinois named after legendary University of Georgia football coach Vince Dooley, were assigned to a 65-mile stretch of what he and other troopers referred to as the zipper. I-75 was the main pipeline for drug traffickers from Miami to points north. It was Taylor and Dooley's job to stop and arrest the traffickers and impound as many drug shipments as possible. Although the trooper and his canine partner had been enormously successful by consistently breaking records for seizures of narcotics and cash, they only nabbed a small fraction of what was actually being smuggled.

As the trooper parked his vehicle on the east shoulder of the northbound lanes, he noticed the headlights of a distant car in his rear-view mirror. At this time of the morning, traffic was light. When he glanced back in the mirror, he could tell that the vehicle was closing fast and obviously speeding. As the car, a black Honda Accord with dark tints, zoomed past him, he estimated its speed to be at least ninety mph. He told Dooley to hang on and fishtailed from the shoulder onto the pavement in pursuit.

He was the only trooper working on I-75 from Valdosta to Tifton, but he used his radio to notify any local agencies of the chase. A Sheriff's Deputy spotted the Honda, got behind it, and turned on his overhead blue lights. When the driver pulled off the roadway, he lost control. The vehicle skidded off the interstate and crashed into a wooded area. The driver of the Accord fled on foot into the brush and the darkness.

By the time Trooper Taylor and Dooley arrived, a makeshift perimeter had been established. Dooley quickly acquired the fugitive's scent and raced directly to his location barking excitedly. He was lying flat in some high weeds and gave up immediately. When they cuffed and patted down the driver, they found a driver's license in his wallet issued to Errol Joseph.

Back at the GHP barracks, Joseph's fingerprints were taken and submitted to the FBI. As it turned out, Errol Joseph was an alias used by a fugitive named Richard Stitt, aka: Death, who was wanted in Virginia for five separate murders. The same Richard Stitt who aligned himself with Boobie during the war in Virginia with the Thomas Family. The warrants were for murders that occurred during that conflict four years earlier.

Since the names Richard Stitt and Corey Mucherson had surfaced in the Amoco murders, it was now apparent that the

Boobie Boys were involved. This was quickly confirmed when the families and friends of both victims were interviewed. It was evidently common knowledge on the street that the Boobie Boys were embroiled in a deadly feud with a group from Overtown, known as Vonda's Gang. This dispute over drug turf had resulted in multiple murders during the past two and a half years. Although the murders had occurred in both the City of Miami and Miami-Dade County, none of the homicide detectives working at either agency had made the connection. The incidents were being investigated as unrelated.

When we finally realized what was happening and researched the cases, the numbers were staggering. There had been at least fifty-two people shot because of the conflict. Thirty-five had died, including a 5-year-old boy. Many of the shootings had occurred in public places, endangering, and killing innocent bystanders. It became apparent that the dismantling of the Thomas Family drug organization did not put a stop to the violence on the streets of

Miami-Dade County as we had hoped. By eliminating the Thomases, Boobie was allowed to become even more powerful and his greed for money and power had resulted in even more carnage.

I took the findings to my boss, Lieutenant Tyrone White. He slowly nodded his head while digesting the memo I had written.

"You're sure these numbers are right?" he asked. I assured him they were.

Tyrone and I had been friends for over 10 years. I was his sergeant when he was a young detective in the Robbery Bureau, and he now supervised me in Homicide. Tyrone was as standup as they come, an outstanding cop, and a pleasure to work with.

A Miami native, Tyrone excelled on the football field at Hialeah Miami Lakes High School and turned his athletic prowess into a full scholarship to Florida A&M University, where he starred on the gridiron for four years. At A&M, he majored in journalism hoping to start a career as a sportswriter when he graduated, but while wandering through a mall one day, a police officer at a recruiting table, handed him an application for the Miami-Dade Police Department. He was hired in 1983 and eventually rose to the rank of Major. Still a gifted athlete, he continued playing football for the MDPD team, Magnum Force.

Tyrone's son, James, was a standout running back at the University of Wisconsin. In 2014, he was the fourth-round draft pick of the New England Patriots. He remained with the Patriots for seven years, playing in three Super Bowls. He is the only player in NFL history to score a touchdown in overtime during a Super Bowl game.[27]

Sadly, Tyrone was killed in a car crash on September 20, 2020. The driver, who was travelling over 100 miles per hour when he hit Tyrone's car broadside, was charged with vehicular homicide.

---

[27] Baltimore Colt Alan Ameche scored an overtime TD during the 1958 NFL Championship game. Not a Super Bowl.

Just as many people remember where they were and what they were doing during tragic events such as the JFK assassination, the toppling of the World Trade Center Twin Towers, or the Challenger explosion, I remember vividly the day I heard about Tyrone's death, and I probably always will. I had taken my grandkids to Universal Studios that day and was sitting on a bench in front of the Harry Potter Castle when my son called me on my cell phone. My son is a lieutenant with the Miami-Dade Police Department and had even worked for Tyrone for a brief time at the Northside District station. When he told me the news, I was heartbroken.

"I'm going to have to run this up the chain," Lieutenant White said. "You should get with City of Miami Homicide and compare notes. The third floor is not going to be happy. As you know, we've been taking a lot of heat in the media about the increase in shootings and murders."

I nodded.

"This would explain a lot though," he said. With that, he plucked the memo off his desk and headed for the captain's office.

I returned to my desk and called John Campbell, the lieutenant in charge of the homicide bureau over at the City of Miami. When I explained to him what our recent intelligence gathering had revealed concerning the Boobie Boys and Vonda's Gang, he said he had never heard of either group. He said that his focus for the past several months had been a narcotics organization known as the John Doe Boys. They controlled the dope trade in the Pork and Bean projects and were responsible for at least twenty murders. I confessed that I had never heard of the John Doe Boys. I suggested that we meet to share information and he agreed.

An hour later Lieutenant White poked his head inside my cubicle. "They want you to prepare some kind of presentation for the command staff that explains what's going on," he said. "They're worried that it will get out that we don't have a handle on it."

"When?" I asked.

"Monday at 2 p.m. in the main conference room." He gave me a knowing smile and walked back to his office. I let out a slow, deep breath of air. What had I gotten myself into?

Putting together a slide presentation in 1998 was no easy task. There was no PowerPoint readily available back then, so it meant using a slide projector with a revolving carousel on top that held a stack of 35mm slides. Our photo lab did not have the capability to produce slides from photographs, so an outside vendor had to be used. I collected as many crime scene pictures as I could, many of them very graphic, and created charts to visually explain the bloodshed that was occurring on an almost daily basis in Miami-Dade County. I took my materials to a *Foto Master* store at the nearby *Mall of the Americas* to be processed into slides.

When I walked into the main conference room on Monday, I was surprised to see an overflow crowd. All the seats at the huge mahogany conference table were occupied by command staff personnel, and the walls of the room were lined with the lesser peons who were standing. I quickly noticed that the Director, Deputy Director, and several of the Division Chiefs were already seated in the high-backed dark green chairs, as were the District Commanders of the affected districts and their underlings. It was a packed house.

For thirty minutes, I explained the drug war and how it was impacting the streets of Miami-Dade County. I emphasized the wanton violence and how the use of military-style weapons put every street cop in grave danger. I clicked through slide after slide that showed the victims who had suffered the savage effects of the AK-47s. One of the slides depicted the mutilated body of 5-year-old Michael Frazier who had been riddled with 7.62x39 mm bullets. I must admit the slides were brutal and tough to look at. I also displayed photos that showed how the 7.62 round would pass through a bullet proof vest or a Kevlar

SWAT helmet like a hot knife through butter.

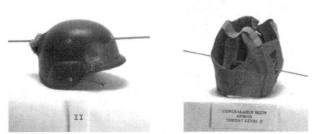

Figure 8. SWAT helmet and vest that were easily penetrated by a 7.62x39 projectile. (Author)

I concluded with a slide that listed the names and ages of the dead who were the victims of this senseless conflict over drug turf. I intentionally left the slide up on the screen and sat down. The room was completely silent. I scanned the faces of those seated at the conference table and saw them looking at each other with obvious concern. They got it. They had been around long enough to know that this was serious. Dire, in fact.

The first to speak was Sergeant Pete Coraddo from SRT (SRT is Miami-Dade's version of SWAT). Pete and I had known each other since the 70s when we worked together in uniform.

"Tony's right," he said. "An AK round will penetrate a tactical SWAT vest with ease. A ceramic shock plate may stop the first hit, but it will crack it...the next rounds will go straight through. And a metal shock plate? Forget it. It won't even slow it down. If any of our uniform guys get in a firefight with these assholes who have these kinds of weapons, they won't stand a chance."

More silence. Finally, the Director glanced in my direction and said, "Thank you, sergeant. You've given us a lot to think about. The command staff will remain and everyone else is excused." Those of us who were lesser in rank filed out of the conference room and back to our cubicles.

The next day, when I walked into the Homicide squad room, Lieutenant White met me. "The captain wants to see us," he said. I followed him into Captain Angus Butler's office. Captain Butler was on the phone when we walked in. He smiled, waved us in, and motioned for us to take a seat. While I waited for him to finish his phone call, it occurred to me how fortunate I was to work for these two men. I had the greatest respect for both of them.

"Well," Captain Butler said as he hung up the phone and looked at me, "They want you to form a task force to go after these drug gangs and put them out of business. You can hand pick your team, and you will be out of the homicide rotation until further notice."

This was not what I expected to hear. Lieutenant White sat across from me with a big smile on his face. "You kind of set yourself up for this," he said.

We had both been on task forces before in the Robbery Bureau and knew that the pressure to produce results when a task force is created is enormous. On the surface, this looked like a no-win situation. The homicides and shootings would be difficult, if not impossible, to solve because witnesses notoriously refuse to come forward when drug gangs are involved. If the killings continued unimpeded, the task force would be blamed.

All of this raced through my mind as Captain Butler continued, "The Director would like to get the Feds involved. If you know anyone you trust, get me the names, and the Director will reach out with a request."

As Lieutenant White and I walked back toward my cubicle, he was still grinning at me. "I guess you're going to be under a hot white spotlight now," he said. "Hopefully, you don't get burned by it."

I knew exactly what he meant.

I spent the next several days gathering intelligence on both crews and choosing the task force personnel. Picking the principal investigators was easy. I chose four detectives I trusted implicitly and whom I knew to be entirely self-motivated. Detectives who would totally immerse themselves in the case and get results. They were Jeff Lewis, Mike Hernandez, Chuck Clark, and Joe Malott.

Jeff, Mike, and Chuck had worked with

me in the Robbery Bureau for a dozen years, and I knew them to be exceptional investigators with strong work ethics. When I transferred to Homicide, I encouraged all three to follow me there. Joe had been on my homicide team for the past several years and was cast from the same mold.

I was not naive. I knew that this was going to be an exceedingly challenging assignment and that we might not be successful. But I also knew that if we were to succeed, it would be these four dedicated cops who would make it happen.

When I summoned them into the conference room to tell them they were now assigned to the newly formed North End Task Force, they stared at me like a group of cows looking at a new gate. They hadn't expected it, but after the initial shock wore off, they declared they were all in.

During the next week, we had multiple strategy sessions trying to plot the best course of action. We all immediately agreed that we had to stop the violence. We had to stop the killing. We intuitively knew that trying to solve the murders would take too much time and that if we just focused on making the homicide cases more people would die. Therefore, we decided to first identify who the main players were in each group and just get them off the streets, even if it meant putting them in jail for misdemeanors or traffic violations.

When we researched the criminal backgrounds of each of our targets, we found our answer. The lieutenants and enforcers in both organizations were career criminals with violent pasts, as you might expect. All of them, it seemed, had prior arrests for gun charges, such as armed robbery, carrying a concealed firearm, possessing a firearm during the commission of a felony, or possession of a firearm by a convicted felon. These charges were routinely nolle prossed (not prosecuted) by the State Attorney's Office.

In Florida, as in many states, it is illegal for a convicted felon to possess any type of firearm. It is a fairly easy case to prosecute. It requires proving two elements: (1) has the person been previously convicted of a felony and (2) did they possess a firearm. In an alarming number of gun cases that seemed to be open and shut, the state prosecutors had simply dropped the charges with no explanation, allowing these violent offenders to go back on the street.

Knowing that it would be useless to try and re-file the charges with the Miami-Dade State Attorney's Office, we all agreed that our best bet would be to resurrect the cases at the Federal level. The Federal statutes regarding gun possession by a convicted felon are far more severe than they are in the state system. If the firearm was possessed in conjunction with any type of narcotics sale or distribution, the penalty was a stiff 10-year minimum mandatory sentence.

We were convinced this would work. Reviving the old gun cases could be done quickly, with minimal time spent re-investigating them. They were basically ready to go. This would accomplish our goal of quickly getting the worst members of each crew locked up and off the streets.

I explained our game plan to Lieutenant White, and he nodded vigorously. "I like it. Let me run it up the chain to the third floor and see what they say. To do this right, you're probably going to need someone from ATF to assist you. And from DEA to work the dope angle," he said.

He was right. Especially about the dope aspect. None of us had ever worked narcotics before. Jeff Lewis knew just the right names we should ask for. He had worked on a couple of cases with a DEA special agent named Lenny Athas. He said Lenny would be prefect. Before being hired by DEA, he was a Maryland State Trooper who had worked street narcotics in Baltimore. Jeff also knew an ATF agent who had been assisting the Robbery Bureau by the name of Carlos Canino. I wrote both names on a piece of paper and delivered it to Lieutenant White.

"L-T, could you check and see if we could get these two Feds assigned to the task force?" I asked.

Three days later, it all came together. I'm not sure what kind of strings were pulled, but Lieutenant White informed me that both Agent Canino and Agent Athas were being detached to the North End Task Force.

He also told me that our timing couldn't have been better regarding the firearms cases. The Attorney General of the United States, Janet Reno, had been taking a lot of heat as of late. She was being accused of being too "pro guns" by the anti-gun lobby. In order to deflect this criticism, and appear tough on gun crimes, she announced an initiative to remove illegal firearms from the nation's inner cities.

Prior to being named the Attorney General of the United States, Reno was the Miami-Dade County States Attorney. It was her office who was so soft on gun crimes and dropped the cases in the first place. Quite a paradox.

Lieutenant White said that Assistant United States Attorney Chris Clark would be at our disposal for the filing of any federal firearms-related charges. The Feds have a penchant for coming up with unique names to identify their investigations. Ours was dubbed "Operation Boobie Trap."

That evening, the five of us met with Chris Clark at his condominium on the Miami River. Chris is featured in the 2021 three-part Netflix series, Cocaine Cowboys: The Kings of Miami. He practically narrates all the episodes. The documentary profiles two of the most famous drug kingpins in South Florida history: Sal Magluta and Willie Falcone. The pair were accused of smuggling over seventy-five tons of cocaine into the United States and amassing an illegal fortune of $2.1 billion in cash and assets. Chris is the Assistant United States Attorney (AUSA) who prosecuted them. Both were found not guilty after a lengthy trial.

The case against them was rock solid and the not guilty verdict was totally unexpected. It was later learned that the foreman of the jury had been bribed. He received half a million dollars to sway the rest of the panel. He was eventually convicted and received a 17-year jail sentence. Falcone was retried for a single count of money laundering and found guilty. He was sentenced to 20 years in Federal prison. Magluta was charged with multiple counts of money laundering and bribery. He was also convicted and sent to the Super Max prison in Florence, Colorado for 205 years.

When we briefed Chris about the on-going drug war and our desire to utilize the Federal firearms laws to stop the mayhem, he immediately agreed with the plan.

"But" he said. "You should know that you have so much more here. I do drug cases, too. This would be a perfect CCE (Continuing Criminal Enterprise). You could include the murders as predicate acts. You wouldn't even have to prove who did them. Just show that they were committed to further the criminal enterprise. It would take a lot of work to put together, but it could be done."

I looked at my four handpicked investigators. I could tell they liked what they were hearing. And so, did I. We were all wired with a strong desire to succeed. The prospect of making cases and putting the bad guys away is what drove us. What Chris had just laid out, the CCE, sounded like the perfect way to crush the Boobie Boys and put them in prison forever.

CHAPTER 7
Vonda

Avonda Dowling was born in 1963. In high school she was bright, slender, tall, and athletic. She excelled in basketball and was named to the All-County girls' basketball squad during her senior year. Known as "Black Girl" or "Vonda" to her friends, she was an admitted bisexual with multiple boyfriends and girlfriends. Over six feet tall, she appeared even more towering due to her beehive hair style.

Her father, James Dowling (AKA Big Jake), was a ranking and influential member of the International Longshoremen's Union at the Port of Miami. As soon as Vonda turned eighteen, she was issued a union card for Local 1416, and started working on the docks with her four brothers.

She also became a thief. She led a gang of teenagers who would storm enmasse (6 to 10 at a time) the high-end department stores in Miami, such as *Burdines* and *Jordan Marsh*. The confusion they created allowed them to grab armfuls of expensive dresses off the racks and flee to awaiting vehicles. Eventually security specialists at the stores began alternating the hangars on the bars the dresses were displayed on. By placing the first hanger in one direction and the next hanger in the opposite direction, and so on, it effectively thwarted the rip-offs because the thieves could no longer carry out armloads of clothing.

So, Vonda and her crew changed their tactics. They began driving stolen vehicles through the plate glass windows of the stores at night when they were closed and hauled away the merchandise.

Vonda grew up in the Overtown section of Miami. Originally known as "Colored Town," it is an impoverished area north of downtown Miami that was settled by the mostly Black railroad workers who built Henry Flagler's railroad extension from West Palm Beach to Miami in the 1890s. From the 1920s through the 1950s, Overtown was a bustling community of

50,000 residents and thriving Black owned businesses. It was home to one of the first Black millionaires in the South, Dana Albert Dorsey. Booker T. Washington high school in Overtown was the first secondary school for Black students south of Palm Beach. It was built on land and with funds donated by Dorsey.

The *Mary Elizabeth* hotel in Overtown served as a refuge for Black entertainers in the 50s. Stars, such as, Nat King Cole, Ella Fitzgerald, Louis Armstrong, Cab Calloway, and Count Basie, were hired to perform at the exclusive hotels on Miami Beach (e.g., the *Eden Roc* and the *Fontainebleau)* but were not allowed to remain on the Beach overnight. They would return to Overtown each evening and stay at the *Mary Elizabeth*. These same artists would also perform free concerts at the famous *Lyric Theater* in the center of Overtown.

In the 1960s, the construction of two expressways demolished most of Overtown and displaced thousands of its residents. When they were built, the

Dolphin Expressway (I-395) and I-95 both cut right through the heart of Overtown. Today, the area is economically destitute, and crime ridden.

Vonda was arrested for larceny and possession of stolen property on several occasions, but she soon advanced to more violent crimes. While still working at the Port, she began "slinging" dope for prominent Miami drug kingpin Bunky Brown. Bunky owned the Magic City lounge and controlled all the drug trade in Overtown. It was rumored that Bunky acquired the money to start his narcotics business from two armored car robberies he perpetrated. The robberies supposedly netted him more than $200,000, the equivalent of $1.3 million in today's money. He is the original philanthropic Miami drug lord that others like Ricky Brownlee, Isaac Hicks, and Boobie sought to emulate.

On May 12, 1984, Vonda married Jerry Jackson who was also a longshoreman at the Port of Miami. (Together, they had two children, Jervante and Vonshari. Jervonte would grow up to play college football at Florida Atlantic University and was signed as a defensive tackle by the Philadelphia Eagles in 2009. He also played for the Jacksonville Jaguars and the Detroit Lions).

Vonda and Jerry Jackson rose in the ranks of the Bunky Brown narcotics organization and found that the dope business was far more rewarding than working on the docks, so they gave up their jobs at the Port and began working exclusively for Bunky. They did maintain their connections at the Port, however, which provided a steady source of illicit cocaine. When Bunky and Jerry Jackson were both sentenced to lengthy Federal prison terms, Vonda took over the distribution of dope in an area of Overtown known as "the Swamp."

Of course, this invited takeover challenges from those who perceived a woman as too weak to maintain control, but the usurpers quickly found out that Vonda was tough, fearless, and unwilling to back down. She was arrested numerous times for aggravated battery. One arrest involved a victim whom she had beaten severely with a baseball bat. Leaving him bloodied, Vonda drove around the block and returned to where the victim was lying on the sidewalk moaning. She beat him again with the bat until he was unconscious.

Another arrest took place when Vonda was stopped by the police fleeing from the scene of a shooting. The victim had been shot multiple times. Police searched Vonda's purse and found a revolver that had been recently fired. The victim survived but refused to identify his shooter or press charges. In another dispute, she used her red Cadillac to run over one of her "servers" who had shorted her money.

Even though she had developed a reputation as someone not to be trifled with, she also chose to surround herself with several cold-blooded enforcers. One of these was Robert Lee Sawyer (AKA Rah-Rah).

When Michael Hollis (AKA McBride), also of Overtown, tried to take control of one of Vonda's drug holes, she hired Rah-Rah to kill him. Sawyer concealed himself with a high-powered rifle on a rooftop opposite McBride's apartment one morning and waited. As McBride stepped out onto his balcony to enjoy his morning coffee, Rah-Rah blasted him in the chest, killing him with a single shot. Vonda paid Rah-Rah $10,000 and a half kilo of cocaine for the hit.

A month later, Rah-Rah shot Peter Charlston in the stomach and Jake Brown in the chest, both at the behest of Vonda. Rah-Rah was arrested for the murder of McBride. In a plea deal which included the two other cases he was sentenced to 10 years in prison.

Figure 9. Vonda Jackson, AKA Avonda Dowling, AKA Black Girl (Author).

Keith Biggens met Vonda Jackson and her sister Paula (AKA Coco) in 1988 through Benjamin Bryant. He immediately began a sexual relationship with Coco and assisted the two women with the distribution of narcotics to an outlet in Macon, Georgia run by Bryant and Curtis "Sissy" Thomas. When Bryant died of a drug overdose, the operation was shut down.

Benjamin Bryant expired on April 24, 1989, after he went on a drug-fueled rampage in a Carol City neighborhood. Barefoot and armed with a machete he attacked a family in their home at 8:30 in the morning. He forced an 18-year-old woman into a bathroom where he cut her repeatedly with the machete and tried to rape her. The teenager's father and brothers broke down the locked door and subdued Bryant who stopped breathing while being handcuffed by the police. Today, his death would undoubtedly be classified as a case of excited delirium due to cocaine; however, in 1989, this cause of death was not widely known.

Curtis Thomas was a homosexual. Hence the nickname "Sissy." On Christmas Day, 1992, Vonda threw a combination birthday and "coming home from prison" party for Errol Sawyer (Rah-Rah's brother) at her duplex on Northwest 50th Street. Sawyer had been locked up for six years in state prison. He was caught with cocaine supplied by Vonda, but he never ratted her out.

James Powell (AKA Short Man) was standing in the kitchen of the duplex when he saw Thomas near the front door. He remarked to Vonda, "I'm going to rob that faggot," pointing at Thomas.

Vonda watched as Short Man placed a gun to Sissy Thomas's head and cocked it. He then demanded that Thomas relinquish all his jewelry. When Thomas refused, Short Man shot him in the leg. Thomas grabbed the gun and jerked it from Short Man's hands. He turned the gun on Short Man and shot him three times in the chest.

Thomas ran into the duplex. Vonda directed him to a back bedroom closet where she told him to hide. When the police and fire rescue units arrived, Short Man was pronounced dead on the scene. No arrests were made.[28]

Short Man was the half-brother of the twins Leonard (Bo) and Lenard (Nard) Brown. He was also Boobie's first cousin. All three vowed to avenge the killing. Five years later, Curtis Thomas was gunned down by Bo and Nard on the dance floor of Studio 183, a nightclub in Carol City.

---

[28] From a statement taken by the author from Vonda Jackson at the Women's Detention Center in Miami.

Even though the drug connection in Macon, Georgia ended, Keith Biggens continued his association with Vonda and her sister, Coco. Keith was one of the few people in Miami who knew how to "whip" powdered cocaine while converting it into crack. The whipping process expanded the volume of cocaine and therefore enlarged the profit margin considerably. By whipping the cocaine, he was able to extract an additional twelve ounces from each kilo, which increased Vonda's earnings by $7,200 per kilo or more. Many dealers at the time would use powdered "blow up" which could be purchased at local head shops to increase the volume of the coke artificially. This was not as efficient as whipping it though.

Biggens whipped cocaine into crack for Vonda for five years until he broke off his relationship with Coco. During this period, he cooked six to eight times a month, and each time, he cooked at least two kilos (sometimes three) into crack cookies. Biggens was aware of Vonda's connection with the docks and knew she always had a steady supply of product from the Port of Miami.

Keith Biggens was an interesting character. He spent a lot of his adult life in prison but was always well connected to the streets, even from the inside. I began talking to him while I was in the Robbery Bureau. He would call collect from whatever prison he was in and would talk for hours if I let him. He wasn't what I would call a snitch as much as a gossip. He loved to talk about the streets and the gangster lifestyle, which he admired greatly. He was smart and articulate. He was a great storyteller….a natural raconteur. If I needed to ask Keith a question regarding a case, I would call his mother who would relay my message to him. If his mother was not home, (she spent a lot of time in church), I would leave a message on her answering machine. The problem was that on her outgoing message, his mother would sing three full stanzas of Amazing Grace. She had a beautiful voice, but it took a whole two and a half minutes of waiting and listening before I could leave a message.

When Bunky Brown was sent to Federal prison for life and Vonda took over his organization she copied the cordial relationship he had fostered with the community. Like Bunky, she sponsored athletic teams in Overtown, buying uniforms and equipment every year. If a baseball or football field needed renovating, she would foot the bill. At Christmas and Thanksgiving, she passed out turkeys. On Easter, Vonda would dress in a bunny costume and hand out Easter baskets. She would also buy matching bunny costumes for all the young girls in Overtown and throw a big party for the residents.

Figure 10. Every Easter Vonda purchased bunny costumes for the youngsters in Overtown. (Miami Times)

If someone was short on money for their rent or electric bill, Vonda would pay it. If kids needed shoes for school, Vonda furnished the money to buy them. She would rent a van and take the local children to Disney World or out for pizza. She would sponsor dances with local DJs for graduation parties. It was hard to find anyone in Overtown who had a bad thing to say about Vonda.

In addition, she took care of those who worked for her. When Roger Davis was killed at the *Amoco* gas station on NW 62nd Street, it was Vonda who paid for his funeral. And at the cemetery, she slipped the family an envelope full of cash.

When Raymond Rich was killed, and her half-brother wounded by rival dope dealers it was Vonda who paid for Rich's funeral. Then, on the one-year anniversary of his death, she rented five stretch limousines to transport family and friends to his graveside for a memorial service.

She was also known for throwing lavish parties to reward her workers and to increase her clientele. Her soirees were extravagant and well attended. They were often held at the plush Omni Hotel or at a large stately house on Biscayne River Drive she had built with the proceeds of her drug sales. Guests were served a panoply of assorted drugs. Sterling Silver trays heaped with huge mounds of powdered cocaine were passed around like hors d'oeuvres. Many of the parties ended in sex-orgies that included both heterosexual and homosexual couplings.

In early 1995, the Matchbox projects were condemned and demolished. This created a huge dilemma for Boobie. Many of those loyal to him were displaced to other government housing projects throughout north Miami-Dade County. His base of operations was gone. He had to acquire new territory to not only insure his cash flow but to show his dominance and display his power. A drug kingpin can't be perceived as weak and needs to control "turf" in order to show how powerful he is. Weakness invites overthrow attempts by rival groups.

Initially, he decided to take over drug holes controlled by the John Doe Boys, but they resisted with such ferocity that he abandoned the idea. A shootout between the Boobie Boys and John Doe Boys occurred in the parking lot of Studio 183, it resulted in multiple victims who were critically wounded on both sides. After that he, and Corey Smith (AKA Bubba), the head of the John Does, met and agreed to a truce. He also knew it would be a mistake to move into Opa-Locka and challenge Ricky Brownlee. So, he decided to test the waters in Overtown.

March 23, 1995
3 p.m.

Marvin Rogers's wife worked at a small neighborhood grocery store on NW 2nd Avenue in Overtown. Rogers and several of Boobies flunkeys began selling crack in front of the store. When Vonda learned of their new enterprise, she sent a messenger telling them to shut it down. They refused.

Because his wife was employed in Overtown, Marvin Rogers spent a lot of time there. He was lifting weights in the courtyard of the Rainbow Housing Projects shortly after he had been warned to close down the dope hole on 2nd Avenue. Two gunmen snuck up behind him while he was curling dumbbells and shot him multiple times. He recognized one of the shooters as Edward Fortner, who he knew worked for Vonda. He was taken to Jackson Memorial Hospital in critical condition.

There are a number of nightclubs, bars, and strip joints that are intertwined in the

Boobie Boys story. One, certainly, is the Club Rolexx. Another is Studio 183.

Studio 183, located at NW 27th Avenue and 183 Street, is a former JC Penney department store. It was transformed into a 51,000 square foot entertainment complex by its owner, Ezekiel Hodge.

The interior included a multi-purpose hall called Studio 183; a flashy discotheque christened Miami Nights; and a cozy jazz nightclub named the Jazz Room. It was frequented by many entertainment luminaries visiting Miami, including NBA and NFL players. It also attracted the local gangsters. It was rumored that Boobie had invested heavily in the club as a way to launder his narcotics money.

Figure 11. Studio 183 nightclub in Carol City (Author).

The day after Marvin Rogers was shot, Boobie and several members of his crew, including the Twins and Efrain Casado (AKA E-4), visited him in the ICU. They were furious. They knew Vonda's Gang was responsible, and they promised revenge. Boobie had recently formed an alliance with E-4, who he had met years earlier in Youth Hall. E-4 commanded his own crew who were mostly childhood friends that grew up in the Little River area of Miami. Boobie and E-4 agreed to join forces to supplant Vonda and take over the lucrative drug market in Overtown.

After the others had gone, Boobie stayed at the hospital standing beside Marvin Rogers beside. He was very close to Rogers. He considered him a brother. As he stared at the tubes that drained fluid from his lungs and stomach, his hatred for Vonda and her people grew.

When he left the hospital that evening, he met the Twins and E-4 at Studio 183. They were standing near the bar when Nard pointed to the dance floor. "Look!

There go those niggers who work for Vonda. That's some bold shit man, showing up here the day after doing Marvin that way."

There were four of them; Eddie Davis, Davode McLucas, George Donaldson, and Andre McWhorter (AKA Bam). The Boobie Boys could not contain their fury. They confronted them on the dance floor where a pushing and shoving match ensued. Punches were thrown until the club's bouncers broke up the melee.

"Go get the choppers," Boobie told the Twins. "We gonna take care of business."

When the four Vonda Gang members left Studio 183 at 4 a.m., another altercation took place in the parking lot. It was not physical this time, but insults and threats were hurled back and forth. Mario Frazier and his girlfriend, Donneka Hall, witnessed the argument.

A short time later, Frazier was the passenger in his girlfriend's car as she was driving eastbound on the Palmetto Expressway when a primer-colored Chevrolet Lumina passed them. E-4 was the driver of the Chevy, and Boobie was in the front passenger seat. He continued watching as it pulled alongside a wine-colored Impala occupied by the four members of Vonda's Gang. He noticed that both Boobie and E-4 had pulled dark-colored ski masks down to hide their faces. Boobie leaned out of the front passenger window of the Chevy and began firing, what Frazier recognized as an AK-47 at the Impala. The vehicle careened off the expressway and struck a palm tree while airborne.[29]

The Miami-Dade Police arrived and found McLucas, 23, Donaldson, 21, and Davis, 27, dead inside the vehicle. It was unclear if they had died from the gunfire or the crash, but a subsequent autopsy confirmed that all three were killed by bullets. A 9mm handgun was found in the wreckage that was determined to be unfired.

---

[29] From the court testimony of Mario Frazier and from an interview conducted by Det. Mike Hernandez.

Petherina Hannah heard the gunfire and the crash. She was visiting relatives who owned a house on the southside of the service road that runs parallel to the Palmetto Expressway. She jogged to the wreckage to offer help. Inside she saw the mangled bodies of the three victims. In an article published in the *Miami Herald* she was quoted as saying, "I can't forget the blood, the bodies. Jesus Lord three people dying at one time. And they were three boys. I'm the mother of three sons. I hope they catch the people that did it."

Hannah found Andre McWhorter the sole survivor, bloodied, in shock, staggering and rambling near the scene. He had been thrown clear of the vehicle and was uninjured. He kept repeating, "I don't know if I'm hit. I don't know if I'm hit."

Vonda Jackson paid for all three funerals.

Figure 12. Wine colored Chevy occupied by members of Vonda's Gang struck a palm tree after careening off of the Palmetto Expressway. (Miami-Dade Clerk of the Court).

Figure 13. The vehicle was towed to the Medical Examiner's Office where the three bodies were removed. (Miami-Dade Clerk of the Court).

CHAPTER 8
Rah-Rah

When Rah-Rah was sentenced to prison for the murder of McBride, the Twins were 8-year-old "Jits" riding their bicycles. He knew their mother, Susan Hall Gibson, who ran her own dope hole in Overtown. He would pat them on the head and give them candy or small change to buy comic books. By the time he was released from prison 10 years later, the Twins had turned into maniacal killers.

In August of 1996, his friend Wallace Fortner picked up Rah-Rah from the exit gate of Florida State Prison in Raiford and drove him back to Miami. In less than a month, Fortner would be dead---shot and killed by Marvin Rogers and E-4. His body was butchered by AK-47 rounds in retaliation for the shooting of Rogers by Edward Fortner a year earlier.

A few weeks later, another close friend

of Rah-Rah's, Raymond Rich (AKA Boston) was shot and killed by the Twins. He angrily confronted Nard Brown. Nard told him that the murder of Boston was an accident. He said that they were really trying to kill Jamal Brown (AKA Pookalotta) who was Vonda's boyfriend and a lieutenant in her drug organization. They only wounded Pookalotta, Nard said, and Boston was killed by a stray bullet during the attack.

Upon returning home from Raiford, Rah-Rah renewed his relationship with Vonda. Vonda fronted him a kilo of cocaine, so he could get back on his feet. He transported the drugs to Tallahassee where his wife Andrea had family and started his own operation. Within months, he and his wife had established a thriving narcotics distribution network in Tallahassee and Southern Georgia.

Every week, Rah-Rah and Andrea would drive to Overtown to replenish their inventory. Vonda was their sole supplier furnishing them with 3 to 4 kilos on each trip. If they should ever run short, Vonda would send one of her couriers to Tallahassee with an emergency delivery. These arrangements were made over the phone, and the kilos were referred to as "basketballs." The deliveries were usually made by her trusted lieutenants, Jamal Brown (AKA Pookalotta), Famous Johnson, or Andre McWhorter (AKA Bam). Bam, as you recall, was the sole survivor of the massacre on the Palmetto Expressway.[30]

Andrea Sawyer's cousin taught her how to cook powdered cocaine into crack and she, in turn, taught Rah-Rah. Her extended family in the Florida panhandle was utilized to distribute the crack rocks.

---

[30] From court testimony and from interviews conducted with Robert and Andrea Sawyer by the author

Things were running smoothy for the Sawyers until Vonda became embroiled in the battle over turf with the Boobie Boys. Feeling obligated, Rah-Rah drove to Miami to offer his assistance. He had killed for Vonda before, and he would kill for her again if it became necessary.

December 11, 1996
10 a.m.

Famous Johnson walked out of his aunt's townhouse on NW 6th Street toward the black Lincoln Continental that was parked in the driveway. Rah-Rah was driving the Lincoln and had dropped Famous off earlier to deliver an envelope of cash to Famous's aunt. She worked for Vonda, stuffing small plastic zip lock baggies with crack rocks and powdered cocaine. Each clear baggie contained one hit or "bump" and sold for $5 to $15 depending upon the market, quantity, and availability. His aunt's nimble fingers could stuff hundreds of baggies every day and she was well paid for her toils.

As Famous opened the passenger door to get in, he saw two men armed with AK-47s crouched down, quickly moving toward the Lincoln. He dove into the sedan and frantically yelled one word: "DUCK!" Rah-Rah looked back over his left shoulder and saw E-4 and Marvin Rogers in his blind spot. Both raised their weapons and began firing. The windows were blown out in seconds. Famous was hit with a piece of metal trim that snapped off and embedded in his leg. Rah-Rah was cut by flying glass. Rah-Rah backed the Lincoln out of the driveway and floored it. Marvin Rogers and E-4 continued shooting as they sped away. Over one hundred AK-47 shell casings were later collected in the street by the police.

Rah-Rah had been carless. Not fully comprehending the newly formed alliances that had occurred while he was incarcerated, he had talked "too loosely" about the murders of his two friends,

Boston, and Wallace Fortner. He had made several offhanded threats to avenge their deaths and to kill those responsible. Apparently his threats had gotten back to the Twins and Boobie. This placed him directly in their gunsights. His reputation as a stone-cold killer and his loyalty to Vonda made him a hazard that the Boobie Boys felt had to be eliminated. The war was on, and Rah-Rah knew he would have no peace until he killed the Boobie Boys...or they killed him.

Exactly two weeks later, on Christmas Day, Rah-Rah struck back. As E-4, his wife, and their 18-month-old daughter, Elina, were leaving their home on NW 96 Street, Rah-Rah and Famous Johnson positioned their white Ford Taurus rental vehicle behind Casado's Chevrolet Suburban and followed them for several blocks. Rah-Rah had purposely chosen the Taurus because it resembled those driven by Miami-Dade detectives. As they approached the intersection of 35th Avenue, Rah-Rah activated a stolen police blue light he placed in the middle of the dash. Assuming he was being stopped, E-4 pulled his SUV onto a grassy area alongside the roadway.

Rah-Rah, armed with an AK-47, and Famous, with a .223 rifle, jumped out of the Taurus, and riddled the Suburban with lead. Believing they had killed the occupants of the Suburban, they rushed back to the rental car and drove off. Witnesses who observed the entire incident called 911. E-4 and his daughter were rushed to North Shore hospital in critical condition. Incredibly, both would live. E-4 remained in the ICU, clinging to life for several days. Although he clearly saw Rah-Rah shooting at him, he deliberately chose not to tell the police. He planned to kill Rah-Rah himself.[31]

---

[31] From the court testimony of Calvin Bell.

Over the next several months there were numerous attempts on Rah-Rah's life by the Boobie Boys. In October, ten months after the attack on E-4 and his family, Rah-Rah was standing with Yvonne Washington in front of her house on NW 56th Street when three shooters who were hiding across the street behind a black Suburban stepped into the roadway and opened fire. Boobie and E-4 were armed with AK-47s. Nard Brown unleashed several blasts from a 12-gauge pump shotgun.

When the shooting stopped, all three gunmen fled in the Suburban, and 35-year-old Yvonne Washington began screaming, "I've been shot. I've been shot."

Rah-Rah was also hit multiple times, and the two were transported to Jackson Memorial Hospital by Miami Fire Rescue. They were in critical condition, but both would survive their wounds.

It was later learned that Yvonne Washington's 17-year-old daughter was dating Nard and that she was tipping off the Twins concerning the whereabouts of Rah-Rah. By spying for the Twins, she was directly responsible for her own mother being shot and nearly killed.[32]

Rah-Rah was hospitalized for three weeks. Six days after his release, he was driving southbound on I-95 in his mother-in-law's green SUV when two vehicles pulled next to him on either side. He saw Boobie leaning out of the passenger window of a Toyota Camry and shoot directly at him with a Mac 10 machine pistol. Rah-rah was hit multiple times. He also saw E-4 fire into the SUV with an AK-47 and Nard with the pump 12-gauge shotgun. His truck swerved, slamming into the concrete retaining wall dividing the expressway, and he lost consciousness.

---

[32] From the court testimony of Errol Sawyer

He was shot to pieces. His wounds were so severe that he should have died at the scene, but he was again transported to Jackson Memorial Hospital where the Emergency Room staff saved his life.

Jackson Memorial Hospital, also known as "Jackson" or by the initials "JMH," is one of the largest hospitals in the world and is the third largest teaching hospital in the United States. It is renowned for its Miami Transplant Institute, which is the largest transplant facility in the county, performing more transplants than any other hospital. It is home to the Bascom Palmer Eye Institute and University of Miami's Project to Cure Paralysis.

But it is the Ryder Trauma Center that is the crown jewel of the Jackson Health System. The four-story, $28 million, free-standing, 166,000 square foot, trauma center was built in 1992 and is considered by many to be the best in the nation, if not the world. Surgical and medical teams from throughout the United States and the Caribbean as well as from Russia, Japan, England, Italy, and France have visited Ryder to study advanced trauma care.

Gunshot wounds are Ryder's specialty. Because of the high crime rate in Miami-Dade County, the Ryder Trauma Center treats more victims who have been shot than nearly any other similar facility in the country.

"If you have to get shot," said Dr. Tony Nejman, anesthesiologist at Jackson Memorial Hospital's Ryder Trauma Center, "This is probably the best place to do it." It is the Ryder Trauma Center that saved Rah-Rah's life.

Since the JMH Health System and Ryder Trauma Center are public non-profit tax supported facilities, it is ironic, indeed, that the South Florida taxpayers were unwittingly funding the war between the Boobie Boys and Vonda's Gang. None of the members of either faction had insurance or normal jobs. They reported none of their illicit income from the sale of illegal narcotics, and therefore, paid no taxes. They did, however, place a constant burden on the health care system by incessantly shooting each other. Their lives were being saved by the best health care specialists in the world, and they didn't pay a single dime. Rah-Rah alone racked up hundreds of thousands of dollars in medical expenses for which he never saw a bill or paid a penny.

Andrea Sawyer was in the elevator at the Ryder Trauma Center on her way to visit her husband when she heard his name being whispered. She intentionally appeared disinterested as she strained to hear more of the conversation. She was in the back of the elevator, and the two men who were talking quietly to each other seemed to be oblivious to her presence. Although she had never met them, she soon realized that it was the Twins who were in the elevator with her. The same

Twins who had repeatedly tried to kill her husband.

She picked up bits and pieces of their conversation but heard enough to realize that they were trying to locate Rah-Rah. She was able to overhear one of them say, "He's still alive! We got to finish this motherfucker right here." It was also clear that they didn't know what room he was in or even what floor he was on. She overheard them complain that none of the staff would supply them with any information, so they intended to call a cousin who worked at JMH for help in locating Rah-Rah's room number.

Andrea casually got off the elevator on the wrong floor and took the stairway. When she finally got to Rah-Rah's room and told him what she had overheard, Rah-Rah said, "We gots to go," and began removing his IV and a drain tube from his stomach. Andrea protested, but he was adamant. "It's too dangerous here. We have to get back to Tallahassee." It never occurred to him to contact the police for assistance.

On the seven-hour drive to Tallahassee, Rah-Rah nearly died again. He spiked a fever and lapsed in and out of consciousness. Fearing he would not make it, Andrea stopped at the first walk-in clinic she saw. The staff was shocked when they saw the eight festering bullet holes in his upper body, and they immediately called the local sheriff's office. The deputy who responded contacted the Miami Police Department confirming their story that Rah-Rah was a victim, and he was transported to a larger county hospital for treatment.

December 31, 1997
1 p.m.

It took over a month for Rah-Rah to recuperate enough to drive a car. He still had sutures on his wounds and was often doubled over in pain. Even though he was not ready to travel, he knew that he had to meet with Vonda to restock his cocaine supply. He was losing money every day because he didn't have enough product to meet the constant demand for crack in the panhandle and Southern Georgia. So, he placed an order with Vonda for three kilos and reluctantly drove to Miami to pick them up. His wife, Andrea, and her friend from Tallahassee, Dee-Dee, were with him.

Rah-Rah knew he had to be careful. He knew that the Boobie Boys still wanted him dead. He also knew that coming back to Miami was risky. Rumors had gotten back to him that E-4's father, Tomas Casado, had placed a $50,000 bounty on his head.

The only person who was aware that he was coming was Vonda. He drove a nondescript rental car with dark tinted windows and checked into the Embassy Suites by Miami International airport under an assumed name with a fake driver's license. (Both Vonda and Boobie had contacts within the State of Florida driver's license facilities in Overtown and Carol City who would furnish them with valid but fraudulent driver's licenses in any name they chose for a fee of $500). He had already given Vonda the cash for the kilos that were to be delivered to him at the hotel. He planned to be in and out of Miami as quickly as possible, but fate intervened.

At 9:30 a.m., Vonda called Rah-Rah at his hotel. She and Pookalotta had just driven by the Green Gate housing projects on NW 51st Street where they spotted Marvin Rogers in the parking lot with the Twins. She told Rah-Rah that Pookalotta and Bam were willing to go there and "take care of business," but they refused to go without him. He told Vonda that he couldn't do it. He said that he was recovering from his previous bullet wounds, and he still had staples in his stomach.

Vonda would not take no for an answer. She begged him to reconsider. She told him that she would "make it worth his while" and "take care of him." She also pointed out that this may be the only opportunity he would have to kill all three at the same time.

Rah-Rah realized that she was right. This

was a fight to the death. There would be no truce. His only hope of survival was to kill as many of the Boobie Boys as he possibly could. So, he agreed.

Rah-Rah drove his Mazda 626 rental car to Vonda's duplex on NW 50th Street where he met Bam and Pookalotta. Vonda furnished the weapons; a Ruger 9mm pistol, a Heckler & Koch .223 rifle, and an AK-47. All three changed into black Dickie outfits that Vonda also provided. Their plan was simple: sneak up on the parking lot and kill as many of the Boobie Boys as they could.

The Green Gate housing project was only four blocks from Vonda's duplex. When the Matchboxes were condemned and torn down, many of the residents loyal to Boobie were displaced and relocated to the Green Gate. It was much smaller than the Matchboxes and was surrounded by a 6-foot wrought iron fence that had been painted green, hence the name. Some residents referred to it as "the Little Matchboxes."

They parked the rental on the north side of the complex. Due to his injuries Rah-Rah was unable to cock the AK-47, so Pookalotta pulled back the charging handle and chambered the first round. Bam was armed with the H&K 360 and had to help Rah-Rah over the fence. He moaned in pain as he toppled to the other side. Bam passed both rifles through the fence to Rah-Rah, and he quickly hopped over himself with no trouble.

Walking silently through the breezeway, they saw Marvin Rogers with his back to them talking on a cell phone. As they inched closer, Rogers noticed them and tried to run across the parking lot. Bam fired one shot and hit Rogers directly in the back. With that first shot, Bam's rifle jammed, so Rah-Rah ran up to where Rogers was lying on the pavement and shot him repeatedly with the AK from fifteen feet away. He leaned closer to Rodgers and fired one last round into the back of his head and watched as his face exploded leaving a gaping hole where his nose, eyes and mouth used to be.

Rah-Rah glanced up and saw the Twins and Johnathon Hawthorne (AKA Moose), standing on the second-floor landing of the complex shooting at him with handguns. He had known all three since they were toddlers, and now, they were trying to kill him. He yelled to Bam to run while he hobbled behind him trying to dodge the bullets and make it back to the getaway car where Pookalotta was waiting. While trying to climb over the fence, he dropped the AK-47 and needed Bam's help to make it over. They crammed themselves in the rental car, and Pookalotta sped off leaving the AK-47 in the grass near the fence.[33]

When Marvin Rogers's body was autopsied, numerous entrance and exit holes were noted in his chest, face, head, arms, stomach, back, and buttocks. The forensic pathologist described the wound to the back of his head as "an entrance surrounded by a tight pattern of stippling."

---

[33] From the sworn statement of Robert Sawyer

Stippling, or tattooing, is commonly referred to as powder burns, but this is a misnomer. Stippling is created when pieces of unburned and partially burned gun powder become tiny projectiles and embed themselves into the skin. The pieces of gunpowder are propelled out the muzzle of the barrel along with smoke and soot.

In order for stippling to appear, there must be a separation of at least a ½ inch between the end of the barrel and the skin. The small projectiles of gunpowder will only travel with enough velocity to puncture the skin from about 2 to 3 feet away. It depends on which type of gun and cartridge are used, of course, but three feet is generally considered the limit. The closer the barrel of the gun to the skin the tighter the pattern will be. The further away the larger the pattern.

If the gun muzzle is 6 to 10 inches away from the skin, there may also be a deposit of soot on the wound. Soot is created by the combustion of gunpowder. Soot is easy to differentiate from stippling…soot will wipe off, stippling will not. It is possible for stippling to penetrate short hair and even thin layers of clothing.

The autopsy report listed twenty-three separate entrance and exit holes in Marvin Rogers carcass. Most of the wounds were described as perforating, which means the bullet entered and exited the body. A few others were described as "penetrating." Penetrating wounds have no exit, and the projectile remains in the body. Many of the penetrating wounds were catalogued as "shored wounds." Shored or supported wounds are created when the projectile is stopped by some type of barrier and not allowed to exit. The concrete pavement in the parking lot, on which Rogers was lying, stopped the energy of the bullets and caused them to remain just below skin level. Shored wounds are typically seen in cases where the victim is executed from close range while lying on a firm surface.

Determining what is an entrance and what is an exit wound can be tricky, but most of the time it is fairly straightforward. Entrance wounds are round and bleed less than exit wounds, which tend to be more irregular in shape and bleed profusely.

An entrance defect is encircled by an abrasion collar and bullet wipe. The pink abrasion collar is caused by the impact of the bullet when it strikes the skin. Because the skin is elastic, the hole will be slightly smaller than the bullet itself.

"Bullet wipe" is the sludge that clings to the bullet as it passes down the barrel. This sludge can include lubricant, propellant by-products, soot, lead vapor, and smoke. As the bullet passes through the skin, this "gunk" wipes off and leaves a black or grey ring. Stippling, abrasion collar, and bullet wipe are all indicative of an entrance wound.

Figure 14. The body of Marvin Rogers lying in the parking lot of the Green Gate housing projects. (Miami-Dade Clerk of the Court).

After dropping off Pookalotta and Bam, Rah-Rah met Andrea, and her friend Dee-Dee at the Embassy Suites. They decided to lie low and checked into a different hotel on Biscayne Boulevard. Rah-Rah called Famous Johnson and warned him to stay off the streets. He told him that he had just killed Marvin Rogers and that the Boobie Boys would be after him.

The next day Vonda delivered the kilos of cocaine Rah-Rah had ordered, and she gave him an extra $12,000 for carrying out the hit. As soon as he received the cocaine, he fled Miami with Bam, Andrea, and Dee-Dee. They drove to Tallahassee, but Rah-Rah knew that Boobie's tentacles extended everywhere and that now he would never be safe.

That same day, New Year's Day 1998, Boobie counterattacked. Pookalotta and Vonda's brother, Rick Delancey, pulled into the driveway at Vonda's duplex when Boobie, the Twins (Bo and Nard) and Shotout (Linard Albury), opened up on them with AK-47s. The fusillade of bullets from the four rifles laid waste to the duplex and the vehicles that were parked in front. Both Delancey and Pookalotta were hit numerous times. One of the bullets severed Pookalotta's spine, and he was immediately paralyzed from the neck down. He remained a quadriplegic and confined to a wheelchair for the rest of his life. As Vonda put it, "He can't even wipe his own ass."[34]

---

[34] From an interview conducted with Vonda Jackson by the author.

Figure 15. Jamal Brown, AKA Pookalotta. (Author)

Several hours later, Famous Johnson drove by Vonda's duplex and saw three Fire Rescue vehicles and half a dozen police cars. He didn't stop but continued driving. While he was heading back to Overtown, he was forced off the road by a black Honda with dark tinted windows. A lone gunman, wearing a black ski mask, leaned out of the back passenger window with an AK-47 and strafed the side of his car. He was unharmed but the message was clear. The war was escalating.

Funeral arrangements for Marvin Rogers were conducted by the Range Mortuary in Liberty City and held at the Jordan Grove Missionary Church. He was 30 years old at the time of his murder and the father of three young children. In a pamphlet, handed out to friends and family at the funeral, was an acrostic of his first name, obviously alluding to his heroics as a member of Boobie's army:

M-memorable times together
A-always fearless
R-real street warrior
V-vicious in battle
I-incredibly brave
N-no limit soldier

Figure 16. Marvin Rogers. (Author).

There were several more attempts made on Rah-Rah's life. Each time he ventured back to Miami to pick up drugs from Vonda the Twins somehow located him. Shootouts in public places between him and the Twins became routine. He knew that it couldn't be a coincidence that they were able to locate him so easily. He knew he was being set up. But by who?

Through his contacts he learned that William Eland was the leak. Eland worked for Vonda but was betraying Rah-Rah to the Twins for money. A few days after learning about Eland's perfidy, Rah-Rah drove by a small neighborhood store located at 7th Street & NW 4th Avenue and spotted William Eland talking on a pay phone. He ordered another member of Vonda's Gang, named Rasheen, to go to the store and kill him.

Rah-Rah parked two blocks away and gave Rasheen a Taurus 9mm pistol. He told him that Eland was on the phone in front of the store and described what he was wearing. He told him to casually walk up behind Eland and shoot him in the back of the head.

Rasheen did exactly what Rah-Rah told him to do. Rah-Rah heard the two gunshots from where he was sitting. Rasheen returned to the vehicle and handed Rah-Rah the handgun and said, "It's done."

When Rah-Rah heard the sirens from the arriving police and fire rescue vehicles, he walked to the scene. He was shocked to see William Eland alive and well and his good friend, Michael Tyson (AKA Bear), lying near the pay phone with a large pool of blood surrounding his head. Tyson and Eland were wearing almost identical clothing. Rasheen had killed the wrong man.[35]

Figure 17. Robert Lee Sawyer - AKA Rah-Rah (Author).

---

[35] From the court testimony of Errol Sawyer and Famous Johnson. City of Miami case number 5319922-X.

CHAPTER 9
E-4

December 23, 1993
11:45 p.m.

Roosevelt Davis had 10 minutes to live, but he would die happy. While walking home from his girlfriend's apartment, he noticed a raucous crowd of 15 to 20 men gambling, playing craps, near 58th Terrace. It was two days before Christmas, and the crowd was in a festive mood. Bottles of whiskey, wine, and beer encased in brown paper bags were being passed around. He joined the group and pulled a wad of cash out of his left pants pocket and another wad out of his sock. "I got this shit on lock down," he told them, meaning he had stolen it. Davis was known to rob local drug dealers and use the proceeds to gamble. He loved to gamble. But he especially loved to "roll the bones" and gamble.

He squatted down and waited patiently. When it was finally his turn to roll the dice, he could do no wrong. He won every pot. As he knelt down grinning and raking in the cash, he didn't notice the two men, one with a University of Miami jacket on and the other with a black hoodie, slowly making their way through the crowd until they were both standing directly behind him.

Roosevelt Davis was jubilant. He clutched a handful of crumpled bills and waved them over his head in the air triumphantly. In a few short minutes, he was able to quadruple his money. He believed that this was his lucky night.

After watching the game for a few minutes, the man in the black hoodie calmly removed a Glock 9mm automatic pistol from his jacket pocket, pressed the muzzle to the back of Davis's head, and pulled the trigger. The gunshot was loud and sent the crowd into a frenzy. Several people displayed guns of their own and began firing into the air, which caused even more chaos. Davis lurched forward face first onto the sidewalk. He was dead...killed instantly. The gunman in the black hoodie continued shooting into his lifeless body. The man in the U of M jacket produced a gun of his own and also shot Davis over and over. Both shooters fled to an awaiting dark blue Ford Explorer driven by Efrain Casado (AKA E-4).

During the attack, one of the bullets ricocheted off the sidewalk and struck 21-year-old Trentius Magaha in the left buttock. He was taken to JMH where he was treated and released.

By the time Miami homicide detectives J.L. Gonzalez and Jose "Pepi" Granado arrived on the scene, it was deserted except for one uniform officer and one crime scene technician. All of the witnesses had bolted, which was not unusual. The victim, Roosevelt Davis, was the only craps player who remained on the scene, which Detective Gonzalez described in his report as follows:

The murder occurred on the northern sidewalk of N.W. 58 Terrace and to the rear of 1240 N.W. 59 Street. The victim is lying on a paved area that is 19 feet wide. There is a 10-foot wrought iron fence that divides the property from the sidewalk. The victim is supine on the sidewalk with his head facing east, his right arm is extended northeast, his left arm is extended south, his left leg is slightly bent and pointing west, and his right leg is crossed over his left and pointing southwest. The victim is wearing a white shirt and blue pants, white socks, and a pair of Converse sneakers. The victim's head is lying in a pool of his own blood, which is draining south. Laying in the pool of blood are two spent 9mm shell casings and a pair of green dice. The victim has been shot a total of 13 times. One shot is to the back of the head.

Figure 18. The body of Roosevelt "Velt" Davis. (City of Miami Police Dept.)

The gunman in the black hoodie who shot first was Benjamin Johnson (AKA Bush) and his accomplice in the University of Miami jacket was Demetrius Wright (AKA Dee). They were lifelong friends who grew up in the Little River area of Miami with E-4 and were part of his narcotics distribution ring. The motive for Roosevelt Davis's murder was revenge.

One month earlier, a home invasion robbery took place at Dee's residence. Dee and his girlfriend were held at gunpoint by two masked men who forced him to open a floor safe. A large quantity of heroin and

$4,000 in cash was taken.

The next day, two armed masked men burst into Bush's apartment, demanding drugs, and money. Bush and Arthur Pless (AKA Plex) were forced to lie face down. Their hands were bound behind them with duct tape. Their girlfriends, Alicia and Shanika, were also duct taped and forced into the shower.

The two gunmen ransacked the apartment searching for cash and narcotics. Both Plex and Bush were beaten and threatened. When nothing was found, the females were taken into a back bedroom, stripped of their jewelry, and raped. The gunmen took turns. One guarded Plex and Bush while the other engaged in various sex acts with the females, including oral sex. Plex and Bush were forced to watch.

All three victims, Plex, Bush and Dee, worked for E-4 and it became obvious to him that the two robberies were committed by the same pair of individuals. The robbers made two serious mistakes. In the robbery/rapes, one of the assailants called the other "Velt," Roosevelt Davis's nickname. And in the other robbery, the heroin taken was uniquely packaged in colorful capsules, which made it easy to trace back to Davis when it hit the streets of Liberty City.

E-4 believed the evidence against Davis was conclusive and vowed that, "Velt won't live to see Christmas." Roosevelt "Velt" Davis was killed two days before Christmas.

The members of E-4's gang were a tight knit group who grew up together, in West Little River, a lower-class neighborhood of Miami. They had been friends since childhood. They attended the same schools together and their families all knew each other. As an act of solidarity, E-4 insisted that every member of his Little River gang have "Street Life" tattooed on them, either on their arms or legs or torso. Bush had Street Life tattooed across his stomach. The artwork was designed by a tattoo artist named Rob who operated a tattoo parlor on 119th Street and NW 17th Avenue. Rob was always paid in cocaine...never in cash.[36]

Little River is bordered on the north by the city of El Portal and on the south by Little Haiti. West Little River extends from Miami Shores to Hialeah. It takes its name from the Little River that runs along its northern border, through the city of Miami, and eventually empties into Biscayne Bay near North Bay Village.

During the early nineties, E-4's rise to drug kingpin was similar to Boobie's. They were about the same age and were both unopposed to the use of violence to further their ambitions. However, E-4 had one big advantage Boobie did not have when he started out. E-4 took over the family business. His father, Tomas Casado, had already been a drug dealer for over a decade.

---

[36] From the courtroom testimony of David Pagan and interviews with Det. Joe Malott and the author.

In the 80s, the elder Casado was an associate of the infamous Albert San Pedro, who at the time, was one of the biggest drug racketeers in South Florida and dubbed "The Great Corrupter."

Alberto San Pedro was born in Cuba ten years before the revolution that led to the dictatorship of Fidel Castro. Before Castro's takeover, the Mafia was a powerful force in Cuba, running all the major hotels and casinos. Alberto's father, Frank, trained racehorses for the Mafia. When he immigrated to Miami in the mid-fifties, he continued training horses at Hialeah Park racetrack and later at Calder Racecourse. He was affiliated with Pasquale "Patsy" Erra, a capo in the Genovese crime family. Erra ran a gambling syndicate in Cuba and owned the Dream Bar on Miami Beach where the clientele included Frank Sinatra and Santo Trafficante.

At Hialeah High School, "Alberto" became Albert. He lifted weights and trained in martial arts and boxing. He became a bully who would "kick anybody's ass" for fifty dollars. After high school, he was frequently arrested for a variety of crimes, ranging from stealing car radios to carrying an illegal firearm to attempted murder. Every time he was arrested, his father's patron and Mafia capo, Patsy Erra would intervene. By the time he was 22 years old, Albert's rap sheet was extensive, but his time spent in jail was negligible.

Patsy Erra and his underboss, Vincent Teriaca, ran a bookie operation that stretched from Miami to New York. They both had sons who were close in age to Albert. Because of his father's connections, Albert started hanging out with the sons, Bobby Erra, and Gary Teriaca.

Even though the pair were in line to inherit the gambling syndicate their fathers ran, they were not your typical gangsters. Both had graduated from the prestigious University of Miami in Coral Gables. They played tennis and golf. They were avid sport fishermen who raced expensive speed boats. Bobby Erra was a frequent golf companion of PGA champion Raymond Floyd. He dated a former Orange Bowl Queen. Gary hung out at the elite Palm Bay Yacht and Tennis club. They were both members of the La Gorce Country Club, the Jockey Club, and the Doral Country Club, which were staid institutions that catered to Miami's high society. They were not "old school mobsters." They were a new breed of "country club wise guys."

Bobby Erra and Gary Teriaca formed a peculiar friendship with Albert. In his book, *How to Get Away with Murder in America*, author Evan Wright describes their relationship this way:

"Albert came into their world as an awkward Cuban kid. His unnerving physical presence and his ferocity were his assets when it came to collecting debts, but he wasn't country club material. No Cuban was. As Italian Americans Bobby and Gary crossed social barriers their fathers couldn't have, but it wasn't yet time for the Cubans. They were still washing ashore on oil-drum rafts. Bobby gave Albert odd collection jobs but barely acknowledged him."

Gary, on the other hand, had a motive for befriending Albert. Albert bragged he had a source for coke: a Bay of Pigs veteran running a smuggling operation. In the 1970s, cocaine was expensive and was a drug only consumed by the rich. Even though Albert had access to cocaine, there was no market for it in working-class Hialeah. That would change in ten years of course, but back then, it was only the wealthy who could afford the white powder. Gary was able to give Albert access to the affluent elite who could afford to use cocaine "recreationally."

Things took off quickly for Albert and Gary. They started out by selling to Gary's contacts at the Pam Bay Club, but word spread, and they were soon doing brisk business at all the country clubs in South Florida. They eventually expanded their operation to another enclave for the rich: Aspen, Colorado. "Within a couple of years, they were moving up to a hundred kilos a month into Aspen. By 1980, Miami-Dade Police intelligence units ranked

Albert and Gary among Dade County's top ten coke distributors."

As the drug money rolled in, Albert changed his persona from street punk to mafioso wannabe. He read the Godfather over and over. He was enamored with the biography of Al Capone. He dressed in expensive Brooks Brothers suits and held court on the stoop of his house in Hialeah where he would conduct his narcotics transactions and, like a true Don, help the newly arrived Cubans with their financial or legal problems. He was 24 years old, and his neighbors referred to him as "the Mayor of Hialeah." His newly acquired wealth allowed him to exert his political influence by bribing officials, at first, in the city of Hialeah, but eventually his graft extended to the county, state, and federal levels.

Figure 19. Alberto San Pedro, "The Great Corrupter." (The Smoking Gun)

In 1975, one of Albert's lieutenants known as El Rubio shot and killed a jealous husband. Albert paid for his legal defense, and El Rubio was acquitted. The family of the dead husband were enraged and attempted to kill Albert. He was ambushed on his front porch and shot multiple times in the hand, face, and torso. One of his testicles was even blown off.

After his near-death experience, Alberto San Pedro became obsessed with the Santeria religion and Saint Lazarus who is revered by the practitioners of Santeria for his purported power over death. He filled his house with statues of St. Lazarus. His mother, who was an ordained Santeria priestess, presided over Santeria rituals and ceremonies, many of which prayed for the safe passage of boats that were smuggling cocaine from the Bahamas to Albert.

The man who would become known as The Great Corrupter used the feast of St. Lazarus, celebrated on December 17th, to distribute his bribes and peddle his influence. He started out by hosting neighborhood cook outs at his house in Hialeah. Members of the Hialeah Police Department were always in attendance as were many of the members of the city council. Council members were given large campaign contributions and sizable donations were made to the Fraternal Order of Police. The mayor and Chief of Police, Whitey Seay, were also frequent recipients of Albert's generosity. He sponsored police judo tournaments and hired off duty officers to guard his mansion. Because of his connections, Albert's brother, John, joined the police department and quickly advanced to the rank of detective.

Eventually the guest list for his Feast of St. Lazarus extravaganzas became so long that he was forced to move from his backyard to the main ballroom at the posh Doral Hotel. The annual event drew over 1,000 people. The dinner tab exceeded $50,000, not counting the political donations and cash given in plain brown envelopes. Inclusion to the party was coveted. It became one of the most popular events on the Miami elites' social calendar, and an invitation was highly prized. It would draw police brass; judges; prosecutors; local mayors; city and county council members; and even members of Congress. U.S. Representative Claude Pepper was a regular attendee. At the height of his political power, Albert's father was named a delegate to the Republican National Convention.

It would all eventually come crashing down. On February 13, 1986, San Pedro was arrested for attempting to bribe two undercover Metro-Dade police detectives. Several weeks after the arrest, it was revealed that investigators had planted listening devices inside of his mansion. Hundreds of hours of incriminating conversations were recorded. Local officials ran for cover. Some resigned, and others announced early retirements.[37]

The Cuban community in Hialeah has always been very close-knit. It was no surprise that Alberto San Pedro and E-4's father, Tomas, became associates in the drug business. The elder Casado integrated many of his family members into the enterprise, including his son Efrain (E-4) and his son-in-law, Rene Texidor. He developed a drug network that was large enough to be lucrative but not big enough to attract the attention of the Feds. He flew under the radar for nearly a decade until he turned over the reins of his organization to E-4.

The violence and mayhem that E-4 was so willing to engage in ultimately led to heightened scrutiny by law enforcement.

---

[37] To learn more about Alberto San Pedro I would highly recommend the book, *How to Get Away with Murder in America,* by Evan Wright.

While Tomas Casado's name was unknown to narcotics investigators, E-4 became notorious and very quickly.[38]

When E-4 took over, his father went into semi-retirement but was always available for advice or to mediate any disputes. In 2004, Tomas divorced E-4's mother, and on Valentines Day, married 45-year-old Carmen Mujica. Less than a month after the wedding, he came home and caught Carmen on the phone with her ex-boyfriend. He calmly walked into the kitchen and began heating several ounces of oil in a skillet. When his new bride asked him what he was doing he said, "I'm going to fry some plantains." After the oil began bubbling and crackling, he walked over to where his wife was sitting and threw the scalding oil in her face. He then used the frying pan to hit her repeatedly on the head.

---

[38] From court testimony of Rene Texidor.

He walked out of the apartment and told neighbors to call 911.

Carmen Mejita spent nine weeks in the burn unit at Jackson Memorial Hospital with third degree burns and a fractured skull. She survived but lost an ear and was totally disfigured because of the attack. Casado was convicted of attempted murder and sentenced to 10 years in Raiford. He died in prison at the age of seventy-three.

The apple didn't fall far from the tree. As a juvenile, E-4 amassed a formidable arrest record. Many of his crimes included violence, but, like most juvenile offenders, he received no serious punishment and was only given an occasional slap on the wrist by being confined to Youth Hall for a few days. His adult criminal history included arrests for aggravated battery, attempted murder, battery on a law enforcement officer, resisting arrest with violence, armed robbery, carrying a concealed firearm, trafficking in cocaine, and escape. By the time he was 23 years old, and Boobie's confederate, he was a hardened criminal with a violent reputation. He had already committed multiple murders to ensure his control of the narcotics being distributed in his Little River neighborhood.

He was also responsible for several murders during dope rip offs. An article published in the *Miami Herald* on February 6, 1994, reported on one of them:

Alvin Kelly, 26, crashed into a fence on Northwest 26 avenue and 99th Street Saturday. Somebody shot him several times while he was behind the wheel. Police have no motive or suspects, said Metro-Dade homicide Lt. Clint Wunderly. Kelly died at 4:50 p.m.

Kelly had just paid E-4 for three kilos of cocaine and thought he was enroute to pick up the drugs when he was shot and killed by Eric Phillips, one of E-4's enforcers.

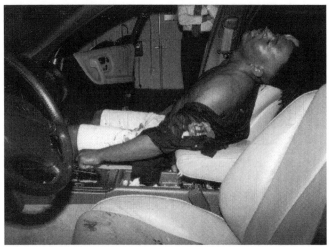

Figure 20. Alvin Kelly was shot by members of E-4's crew during a dope rip off. (Author)

Like Boobie, E-4's drug business was multi-faceted. He delivered both powdered and crack cocaine to Northern Florida and Georgia, because the value of the product increased dramatically when it was transported. And just like Boobie, who controlled the Matchbox housing projects, E-4 had his own domain, the Silver Blue Lake Apartments.

Built from 1962-1964, Silver Blue Lake consisted of four hundred units that all had gorgeous views of an azure blue 80-acre lake. They opened in the summer of 1964 as condominiums and sold for $7995 for a one-bedroom unit. The condominium concept was new and not generally accepted at the time, so due to lackluster sales they were quickly converted into apartments. Since Miami International Airport was only eight miles away, a 10-minute drive at the time, many of the tenants were flight attendants and pilots. Single nurses and doctors from nearby Northshore Hospital also found it convenient.

But by the early-1990s, the Silver Blue Lake Apartments were dilapidated and rundown. The Department of Housing and Urban Development (HUD) stepped in and subsidized the enormous complex as a government housing project. The professionals who once occupied the rental units had been replaced by impoverished families, most of whom sought solace for their miserable lives by smoking crack. This created a cash cow business for E-4 that needed to be defended constantly from usurpers.

One of those was Everette Cooper who

opened a drug hole on the 17th Avenue side of the complex in defiance of E-4 and his crew. Cooper was seated on an old metal milk crate when two of E-4's henchmen, Arthur Pless (AKA Plex) and Ben Johnson (AKA Bush), ambushed him with AK-47s. Plex and Bush later told other members of the gang that Cooper died "with a scared look on his face."[39]

In 1992, construction of the Blue Pointe Apartments was completed. Located just east of the Silver Blue Lake complex, it was much smaller (106 units) and known to locals as "The Colors." Since E-4 already had control of Silver Blue Lake, he initially showed no interest in the Colors, which was loosely controlled by a man named Otis Green. David Pagan (AKA White Boy Dave), however, saw the chance to make some quick money and decided he would challenge Green's monopoly.

---

[39] From the court testimony of David Pagan.

Pagan and E-4 were boyhood friends and with E-4's blessing, Pagan opened his own dope hole in the Colors in direct conflict with Green. To test the waters, he began using two sisters, Brenda, and Rhonda Poole, to sell small amounts of marijuana on the west side of the complex. He then obtained cocaine from E-4, which he provided to the Poole sisters to distribute. One day, while he was collecting money from the sisters, he heard Otis Green remark in a loud voice, "That cracker better not be trying to sell his shit in here."

Pagan had been transporting multiple kilos to Jacksonville at the time and making "big money," but he decided to continue the operation in the Colors "just to annoy Green." As might be expected, he and Green began feuding. It came to a head when he and two of Green's workers exchanged gunfire. Although no one was hit, Pagan decided that the hole was "more trouble than it was worth" and abandoned it.

E-4 was incensed that Green had forced

"one of his people" out and ordered a takeover of the Colors. His workers, organized by Plex, began blatantly selling in Green's territory defying him to retaliate. Plex was already angry with Green because Green owed him $5,000 for drugs and openly refused to pay. When Green pistol-whipped Fat Daddy, one of E-4's workers, and threatened to kill two others, E-4 decided that Otis Green had to die.

May 17, 1995
7 p.m.

Otis Green smiled and waved to the security guard as he drove into the Colors complex. His girlfriend, Alice Gardiner, was seated in the front passenger seat of his gold Nissan Altima. On her lap was her five-year-old son, Mikey. In the back seat was their friend, Brian Gibson.

There was only one entrance and exit to the Colors and it was manned by a security guard, who would raise and lower a gate arm, painted with red and white stripes, to allow access. The exit gate automatically opened when its sensors detected a vehicle.

Green was unaware that a burgundy-colored Honda had followed him in. The Honda was stolen and had been hidden at a warehouse owned by E-4 for just this type of hit. Anthony Brantley was the driver of the Honda. It was also occupied by Plex and Bush. Plex was armed with an AK-47 and Bush with a Mac-10.[40] The weapons had also been secreted at the warehouse along with black Dickie outfits and black ski masks, which all three were wearing.

---

[40] The MAC-10 was invented in 1964 by Gordon B. Ingram the owner of Military Armament Corporation (MAC). It is a blowback operated machine pistol/sub-machine gun capable of firing over 1000 rounds per minute for the .45 caliber version and over 1200 rounds per minute for the 9mm version. The smaller MAC-11 fires 1500 .380 caliber rounds per minute. By comparison, the AK-47 fires 800 rounds per minute. The MAC-10 is notoriously inaccurate at distances over 50 yards. It was used by the U.S. Special Forces (Green Berets) in Vietnam.

E-4 had ordered them to wait in the parking lot of nearby Van E. Blanton Elementary School until he called on his cell phone. E-4, and one of his most trusted lieutenants, Wayne Baptiste (AKA Fat Wayne), were playing basketball on the court in the center of the Colors parking area but they weren't concerned with keeping score. They kept a constant eye on the intersection of NW 103rd Street and 12th Avenue for Otis Green's Altima. As soon as they spotted it, E-4 called Brantley.

Brantley arrived at the Colors just in time to pull the stolen Honda directly behind Green's sedan as it approached the security gate. When the guard lifted the gate to allow Green to enter Brantley followed him, only inches from his bumper, and drove through the gate before it closed.

The plan was to box Green in when he

parked in his regular space, but he unexpectedly stopped and shouted something out of the driver's side window to one of workers on the third floor. Seizing the opportunity, Brantley pulled behind the Altima, and Plex and Bush jumped out with their weapons. Knowing what was about to happen, Brantley quickly backed the Honda up so he would not be hit by a stray bullet.

The gunmen positioned themselves on either side of the Nissan and began firing into the vehicle. Each shooter emptied their thirty round clips into the interior of the sedan. They then ran to the getaway car and fled back to the warehouse where they changed into their regular clothes, hiding the car and guns.

Otis Green died instantly, riddled with bullets. On the floormat at his feet was an automatic pistol that he was unable to retrieve. His girlfriend and five-year-old, Mikey, were transported by Fire Rescue but both died enroute to Jackson Memorial Hospital.

Had he not been slaughtered by E-4 and

his crew, Mikey would have started kindergarten in the fall. Brian Gibson was the only person in the vehicle who survived.

Over fifty shell casings were collected at the crime scene. All the 7.62 casings were tested ballistically and determined to be an exact match with the casings found at the Everette Cooper murder scene.

The killing of Mikey Frazier made national news. Even though the nation was numb by this time to rampant violence and soaring murder rates, the killing of a young preschooler still struck a sympathetic chord and resonated with parents all over the country. Residents of Miami-Dade County demanded answers. It was quickly reported that Otis Green was a major dope dealer, but the public was still outraged over the death of an innocent child.

Even Plex showed some remorse. He claimed he had no idea that a youngster was in the car. When he found out, he told Anthony Brantley's brother, Cedric, "That little boy didn't deserve it, but Otis did." Months later, Plex was still clearly haunted by the death of Michael Frazier and had a tattoo emblazoned on his chest....winged praying hands, with "Mikey" written above them.

Just three months after participating in the triple murder at the Colors, Bush was shot and paralyzed from the waist down. He was standing in front of a bar in the northeast section of Miami when a volley of shots struck him and two others. One of the bullets severed his spine, confining him to a wheelchair for the rest of his life. Bush knew the gunfire was directed at him because he saw the shooter clearly and recognized him, but he refused to tell the police the assailant's name.[41]

[41] From courtroom testimony and interviews conducted with Anthony Brantley by the author and by Detectives Joe Malott and Mike Hernandez. As the driver, Brantley was given immunity from prosecution in exchange for his truthful testimony.

Figure 21. Otis Green was shot and killed at the Colors Apartments. (Miami-Dade Clerk of the Court)

The feigned expressions of regret over the death of Michael Frazier by E-4 and his crew did not stop them from continuing to kill with impunity. If E-4 felt threatened, slighted, or double crossed, he would order that the offending party be rubbed out.

When he learned from trusted sources that a local dope dealer named Johnny Beliard planned to rob one of his stash houses, E-4 and Plex paid Cedrick Brantley $1,000 and a baggie filled with cocaine to kill Beliard. Plex told him he would receive an additional half a kilo of cocaine when the job was done and Beliard (who was also known as Fabian) was dead.

Brantley had a newly acquired Ruger .223 Mini-14 rifle that he had stolen in a residential burglary the day before and figured it would be the perfect weapon to assassinate Fabian. That evening, he hid in an overgrown field next to Beliard's house and waited for him to return home. The rifle only had ten bullets in it when he stole it. He shot seven of them into an old, abandoned washing machine in back of the Diamonds government housing project earlier in the day practicing, so he knew he had to be prudent with the three bullets he had left.

It only took one. When Johnny Beliard pulled his 1958 Chevy Impala into his driveway and exited the driver's side, Cedric Brantley took careful aim and fired. The .223 round, traveling at 3200 feet per second, stuck Beliard in the back of the head. When it exited, it blew his forehead and half of his face away. He was dead before he hit the ground.

Brantley walked from the scene to Plex's house, five blocks away, and told him Beliard was dead. Plex wanted to be sure, so he and Cedric drove by the crime scene, which was now taped off and crawling with police. They then drove to E-4's warehouse where Plex gave Cedrick his half kilo of cocaine. The threat posed to E-4 by Beliard had been eliminated.

Figure 22. Arthur Pless and E-4 paid an assassin to kill Johnny Beliard in his front yard. (Maimi-Dade Clerk of the Court)

May 19, 1996
9 p.m.

Moses Brown had been out of prison for less than a year, but he already had obligations. He had done a three-year stretch for armed robbery, and when he was released, his two "baby mommas" Erica and Ingrid were waiting. Between them, they had four children he had fathered before he was locked up. They were all girls. The oldest was six, and the youngest had just turned four. Since his release, he lived at home with his mother in Bunche Park and spent most days on the streets, hustling for money in any way he could.

Moses primarily supported himself by selling dope in front of a mom-and-pop grocery store in Opa-Locka. Two weeks prior, a Haitian named Don, whom he had met in prison, approached his "spot", and bought several packets of cocaine powder. Don asked Moses if he could introduce him to someone who could buy "weight," meaning large quantities. He told Moses he would pay him for the introduction and any future deals he could broker.

Seeing this as a golden opportunity, Moses contacted *his* supplier, Skinny Kenny. Skinny Kenny told Moses that he was eager to buy as much dope as the Haitian wanted to sell. After several phone calls between Don and Moses, Don agreed to initially sell a kilo to Skinny Kenny. When he arrived with the kilo, Skinny Kenny produced a pistol and attempted to rob Don for the drugs. Don brandished his own gun and shot Skinny Kenny in the back as he tried to run.

Moses had no idea the rip was going to take place, but because he had vouched for Skinny Kenny and set up the deal, Don was now after him. Don's full name was Donald Lorfils, and he was a member of E-4's gang.

Three days after the failed dope rip, Moses received a phone call from Don who wanted to meet and "straighten things out." Moses told his girlfriend that he was apprehensive about seeing Don but felt that he might be able to smooth things over. He admitted to her that he had a bad feeling about meeting with Don. She told him not to go, but he said, "No, I'm going to go and try and fix this." He wrote down Don's phone number on a piece of paper and handed it to her saying, "If anything happens to me, tell the police this is who did it."

Moses left his mother's house and started walking to the store to meet Don. He had gone only a couple of blocks when three cars came to a screeching halt beside him. It was E-4 and his people, there to collect another debt in blood. One of the vehicles was the same stolen Honda that was used in the triple murder at the Colors.

"Fat Wayne" Baptiste and Plex exited one of the sedans armed with AK-47s. Moses stood on the sidewalk frozen with fear as they leveled the rifles at him and began firing. He collapsed almost immediately. Both shooters stood over him and continued firing. His body was mangled by bullets. At the autopsy, more than twenty entrance and exit holes were counted by the ME. Several of the rounds passed through him and gouged out large chunks of concrete from the sidewalk beneath him. One of the projectiles entered the open window of a nearby house. It traveled through the bedroom where an 80-year-old woman had just laid down on her bed. The bullet passed only inches above her face and lodged in the back wall of her home. She said she heard a distinctive whistling sound as it passed over her.

Figure 23. Moses Brown killed near his home in Bunche Park by E-4 and his crew. (Miami-Dade Clerk of the Court)

Another projectile ricocheted off the sidewalk and struck Fat Wayne in the forearm. Within eleven minutes of the shooting, he drove himself to the emergency room of nearby North Shore Hospital for treatment. An X-ray showed the bullet embedded in his forearm, but he refused any further treatment, and left the hospital when the police were called by the ER staff.

(Three years later, Detective Mike Hernandez obtained a search warrant to retrieve the bullet from Fat Wayne's forearm. Several U.S. Marshals took him to the Ryder Trauma Center where Dr. David Schatz from the University of Miami Medical Center performed surgery and removed the projectile. The bullet was introduced as evidence against him in the federal trial charging him with the murder of Moses Brown).

November 5, 1996
3 p.m.

Tarvis Miller had an ankle monitor attached to his right leg. Due to jail overcrowding, some inmates were given the option to remain under house arrest with a monitor for the last four months of their sentences. The device was tracked by a private company who would notify the police if the wearer ventured more than 250 feet from the base unit. The base unit was connected to the landline telephone box on the outside of the prisoner's house. Fortunately for Tarvis, the phone box at his father's residence was on the east side, which meant that his perimeter extended far enough to reach Anita's Bar. This allowed him to sell mini baggies of crack in the parking lot while he was on house arrest. It was a perfect location because any cars southbound on 22nd Avenue could just pull in, quickly exchange money for a small packet, and drive off. It was like a drive-in window for dope.

A big problem with the location though was that it was directly across the street from the One-of-a-Kind Bar. The One-of-a-Kind was owned by Janet Flint, (Michael "Chico" Harper's mother) and was a favorite hangout for both the Boobie Boys and E-4's crew. Nothing annoyed E-4 more than someone selling dope in Little River without his permission. He considered it a personal insult.

When he saw how Tarvis Miller's one-man enterprise was flourishing, he ordered

Willie Simmons (AKA Willie Red) to tell him to shut it down. Willie Red crossed the street and told Tarvis he was on the wrong turf and had to close the hole. Tarvis screamed at Willie Red, "I ain't closing shit! I was born and raised right here! You ain't gonna tell me where I can serve when my house is right there!"

Four days later, Tarvis was still selling. A block away, Willie Red pulled a red Oldsmobile Cutlass, behind Artie's gambling house. E-4 removed an AK-47 from the trunk and got into the rear passenger seat. Willie Red drove the Cutlass south on 22nd avenue as E-4 lowered the rear window and leaned out, firing the rifle repeatedly at Tarvis. Struck twice in the chest, he fell on his back and died with his eyes open.

After the crime scene had been processed, Tarvis Miller's body was loaded into the medical examiner's van and taken to the ME's office to be autopsied. As the van drove away, the ankle monitor alerted the base unit that he had left his restricted area, and the Department of Corrections was notified.

Figure 24. Tarvis Miller killed over dope territory. The ankle monitor can be seen on his right leg. (Miami-Dade Clerk of the Court)

David Pagan (AKA White Boy Dave) and E-4 were lifelong friends, "almost like brothers." Many people thought they *were* brothers. They grew up in the same neighborhood and hung out together since they were toddlers. In the early nineties, at E-4's urging, Pagan began transporting drugs to Jacksonville, Florida.

In 1992, Pagan married Delores Bailey whose brother Nathaniel Gardner, had a thriving dope hole in Jacksonville. E-4 encouraged Pagan to use Delores to transport kilos of cocaine to her brother.

Cocaine that E-4 would furnish.

Pagan and his wife eventually moved to Jacksonville and returned on a regular basis to Miami to purchase kilos of powdered cocaine from E-4. Pagan would realize a profit of $3,000 on each kilo he brought "up the road" to Gardner.

After a brief time, Gardner introduced Pagan to another dealer, named Dexter, who owned a tire store. He began supplying Dexter with kilos. Dexter then introduced him to Jason Stephens (AKA Psycho), who owned a meat market on Moncrete Street. Psycho soon became another one of Pagan's customers. The demand for kilos from Gardner, Dexter, and Psycho was so great that Pagan was forced to hire several of his wife's female cousins as "mules" to deliver the drugs.[42]

---

[42] From courtroom testimony and interviews conducted with David Pagan by Det. Joe Malott and the author.

Psycho and Pagan ultimately had a falling out over money and decided to part ways. Plex stepped in and filled the void by delivering kilos to Psycho that he had acquired from E-4.

Psycho certainly lived up to his nickname. In 1997 he was arrested for the murder of a 3-year-old boy. He killed the child by strangling him to death.

On June 2, 1997, Psycho negotiated a drug deal with Robert Sparrow, Jr. Psycho and three others went to Sparrow's house to exchange money for drugs. As soon as he walked into the house, Psycho produced a 9mm pistol and announced a robbery. He grabbed Robert Sparrow III, who was 3 years and 4 months old, and held him at gunpoint, demanding that his father hand over the drugs.

The boy's mother attacked Psycho trying to free her son, and Psycho struck her on the bridge of the nose with the pistol. He then ejected a bullet from the gun to show that it was loaded. The six occupants in the house, including a 6-year-old girl, were herded into a bathroom. One of the accomplices guarded the bathroom door while Psycho searched the residence for money and narcotics.

Psycho told the victims he was taking the youngster as insurance. He said that if no one followed him, he would release him on the corner. He was about to exit the front door with the child, when Robert Sparrow's half-brother, David Cobb, showed up in a dark green Kia. Psycho forced Cobb into the bathroom at gunpoint with the others and took the keys to the Kia from him.

Psycho's three accomplices were waiting, parked at the curb in a black vehicle. When they realized that Psycho was kidnapping the 3-year-old, they refused to let him in the car and drove off. He therefore shoved the boy into the Kia and sped away.

Seven hours later, the Kia was located in a residential area. Robert Sparrow III was lying face down on the passenger seat dead. The medical examiner determined he had been strangled to death. The autopsy revealed numerous areas of petechia in his eyes and on his face.

Petechial hemorrhages, or petechiae, are pinpoint red dots that appear because of pressure building up in the capillaries and causing them to rupture. They are most easily visible in the white scleral membranes of the eyes, in the conjunctiva of the eyes, or on the underside of the eyelids, but can appear on the skin of the face. They are caused by inconstant pressure and are seen 90% of the time in manual strangulation (also known as throttling). The intermittent squeezing on the throat and releasing of pressure will cause the small vessels to burst.

Manual strangulation in children is hard to detect because the hyoid bone, the cartilage that holds the airway open, is far more flexible in young people than in adults and may not break. A broken hyoid bone is a sure sign of manual strangulation. The older one gets; the more calcification occurs to the cartilage in the throat and the more brittle the hyoid becomes. As one ages, it resembles bone more than pliable cartilage. In a young person, strangulation may be undetectable because the hyoid will bend and not snap. In an older person, say for example 66-year-old Jeffery Epstein, the hyoid will almost always break during throttling (strangulation).

Other signs of manual strangulation are markings that look like half-moons on the deceased's neck. These are caused by the killer's fingernails digging into to the victim's throat when pressure is applied. The medical examiner found small half-moon scratches on young Robert Sparrow's throat as well as petechia in his eyes and on his face indicating that he had been strangled.

During his trial, Jason Stephens (Psycho) claimed that when he left the boy in the car, he was still alive. The twelve-person jury didn't believe him. He was found guilty and sentenced to death.

Figure 25. Jason Stephens --- AKA Psycho, is on death row. (Florida Dept. of Corrections)

CHAPTER 10
Marvin and Prancina

Prancina McIntosh was a few years older than Boobie and grew up with him in Carol City. They were very close, and Boobie even referred to her as his "aunt." Prancina leased a house in northwest Miami-Dade County with her cousin Malcolm Shaw (AKA Rat) who was also Boobie's cousin.

Rat began trafficking cocaine at about the same time Boobie seized control of the Matchbox projects. Rat had a "secret" supplier who always had an ample stockpile of cocaine. He would regularly accommodate Boobie by selling him cut rate kilos but refused to divulge his source, fearing that Boobie would try to rob him.

Prancina assisted Rat by counting the cash proceeds and keeping track of the inventory. In return, Rat paid the rent and all the utility bills. She had twin sons who lived with them. Rat used Prancina's 14-

year-old twin boys, Cedric and Chedric, to deliver packages of cocaine in Carol City, utilizing taxi cabs that he would pay for. In return he would buy them school clothes, stereo equipment, and other expensive gifts. At various times Rat's brother, Sebastian Jacobs (AKA Bess), would assist with deliveries and collections of the drugs and money.

In the early 90s, Prancina started dating a Miami-Dade police officer named Marvin Baker. When Baker visited Prancina, Rat "tested" him by, at first, leaving lines of cocaine on the glass coffee table and then allowing him to see bricks of cocaine in an open duffel bag. Since Baker seemed unfazed by the drugs and made no effort to arrest him, Rat decided Baker was "all right" and began openly displaying cocaine and money in front of him. He eventually proposed to Baker that they could form a profitable partnership by ripping off his customers. Baker agreed.

Using his marked green and white Metro-Dade police vehicle equipped with overhead red lights and clad in his full police uniform, Baker would stop buyers either leaving or on their way to Rat's house. If Rat sold kilos to an unsuspecting buyer, Baker would wait down the street, follow the buyer, and conduct a traffic stop. He would search the vehicle, "impound" the drugs, telling the driver to be on his way. He would then return the kilos to Rat who would pay him a flat fee of $2,000 per kilo.

If Rat knew the type of vehicle a buyer was driving, Baker would stop it enroute to Rat's house and "confiscate" the cash. They would choose their marks carefully. First-time buyers from out of town were frequent targets. They would typically pick buyers who were alone and looked "soft." Someone who would not resist or make a formal complaint.

Boobie found out about their seemingly fool-proof scheme and wanted in. He also provided Baker with victims to rob. They got away with it for years, robbing dozens of individuals without a mishap.

In 1995, Baker teamed up with Trevin Johnson, another Metro-Dade uniformed cop, and conducted similar rip offs for another group of narcotics dealers. Johnson, a former Eagle scout, approached Baker for help because he couldn't keep up. He had too many dopers to stop and steal from.

Everything finally came unraveled when one of the victims complained to Internal Affairs. Through the first victim the IA investigators found dozens of more people who had been robbed by the duo. They obtained a wiretap and discovered additional illegal activities. Finally, they conducted a sting operation that snared both Johnson and Baker. Undercover detectives posing as drug dealers were stopped and robbed by the crooked cops. Each stole a duffel bag containing 4.5 kilos of cocaine and $16,000.

Officers Baker and Johnson were charged with Racketeering in state court and faced life sentences. The prosecution had over 1,500 recorded conversations between the officers and the bad guys that were played for the jury. After an exhaustive four-month trial Baker was acquitted of all charges, even though his co-defendant Trevin Johnson, who pleaded guilty just before trial, testified against him. Baker was the only defendant found not guilty. The six other defendants were declared guilty of Racketeering by the jury. Johnson was sentenced to 25 years in state prison.

Marvin Baker had additional problems, however. It was decided that the rip offs he committed with Boobie and Rat would be included in the Federal CCE (Continuing Criminal Enterprise) case being put together by the North End Task Force.

Marvin Baker was hired as a police officer by Metro-Dade County in 1983. Most of his career was spent in uniform, patrolling the streets of Carol City.

On July 29, 1988, Baker was severely wounded by gunfire as he stood with a crowd of patrons in front of a northwest Dade tavern. Multiple shots were fired at the group as they congregated in front of Mr. B's Lounge. The lounge was in the same shopping plaza as MDPD's North

District sub-station.

Baker's cousin, Causey Bryant, was also hit, along with another man and a woman. All four were transported to local hospitals. Baker was the most seriously wounded. He was struck in the upper leg and lost a critical amount of blood on the scene. Sam Ferguson was shot in the forearm and leg. A bullet lodged in the left hip of the 20-year-old female.

At first, it was thought that Marvin Baker was targeted because he was a police officer. But it was later learned that the gunmen were trying to kill Sam Ferguson. Witnesses identified one of the shooters as Joseph Sweeting (AKA Oomp) who was an enforcer for the Untouchables street gang that operated out of Goulds in the southern part of Miami-Dade County.

Sweeting is a suspect in numerous murders in South Florida, but his most famous slayings occurred in Atlanta at a party following Super Bowl XXXIV. On January 31, 2000, he was with Baltimore Ravens all-pro linebacker Ray Lewis when a fight broke out in the Cobalt Lounge between Lewis's entourage and a group of revelers from Ohio. The fight spilled out into the parking lot, and during the melee, two men from the Ohio party were stabbed and killed.

The day before the murders, Lewis was signing autographs at a Sports Authority and was accompanied by Sweeting. Sweeting purchased three knives at the Sports Authority. One of the knives was a seven-inch Gerber Chameleon II, which is used to gut animals. The autopsy revealed that the wounds sustained by the victims were consistent with that type of knife.

It was a vicious attack. Both victims were stabbed multiple times. Lewis initially claimed he knew nothing about the fight but then changed his story when blood from the victims was found in his limousine. He was wearing a white suit the night of the murders that has never been recovered. It is believed that the suit was blood soaked and was disposed of by Lewis. He blamed his two companions, Joseph Sweeting, and Reginald Oakley, for the deaths of the victims. He even testified against them but did so half-heartedly and both were acquitted. On the stand, he denied much of what he had originally told the prosecutors and investigators. He was allowed to plead guilty to a misdemeanor charge of obstruction of justice and placed on probation for twelve months.

During the murder trial, Ray Lewis claimed that he barely knew Sweeting. That was not true. They were long-time friends and Lewis knew Sweeting's background well. Sweeting did not hide his criminal activities; in fact, he flaunted them. He was an avid supporter of the Miami Hurricanes football team, where Ray Lewis played linebacker. He and the infamous rapper, Luther Campbell were allowed unlimited access to the sidelines during games and threw wild, lavish parties for the players afterward at local bars and strip clubs.

Even though both Lewis and Sweeting served no jail time for the Atlanta killings, Sweeting was furious that Lewis testified against him. He called him a "rat" and refused to speak to him after the trial. In a rap song he wrote about the incident,

Sweeting basically admitted to the murders in the lyrics saying, "If I knew what I know now, it'd have been three bodies."

While dating Baker, Prancina heard persistent rumors on the street that he was a "dirty cop" who would rob people of their money and drugs. She was not convinced until she was present one day when Rat and Baker orchestrated the rip-off of a dope dealer known as Collard Green. Collard Green was stopped by Baker for an alleged traffic violation, and $48,000 was stolen from him. She was present when Rat and Baker split the proceeds. After that, she witnessed many similar incidents.

Prancina and Baker eventually split up and she started dating one of Boobie's close friends, Michael Harper (AKA Chico), whose mother owned the One-of-a-Kind Bar, the hangout for the Boobie Boys. Chico told her that he had filed a formal complaint against Marvin Baker with the police internal affairs section. He said he had been stopped on more than one occasion when Baker stole money or drugs from him. He told her, "I'm tired of getting ripped-off by Officer Baker."

April of 1998, was the last time Prancina spoke to Marvin Baker. He came to the hospital to visit her terminally ill father. She asked him for money to buy a funeral dress and he simply walked out of the room.

Thievery by police officers is extremely rare. Criminals in uniform like Marvin Baker and Trevin Johnson are detested by all good, honest cops who are inescapably tarnished by their misdeeds. Corruption, misconduct, and abuse of power among law enforcement officers is surprisingly uncommon. While it is true that most major law enforcement agencies have had corruption problems, the percentage of law enforcement officers who are "bad apples" is far less than 1% of the more than 800,000 officers in the United States. Lawyers, doctors, and clergymen have higher rates of wrongdoing.

The fact is an overwhelming majority of

officers are principled, trustworthy, and reliable in the face of incredible temptations of the job.

Miami-Dade County has had its share of police corruption. In the 60s, during the term of Sheriff Talmadge Buchanan, dishonesty was rampant. Buchanan and most of his command staff were indicted by a grand jury for associating with bookies, jewel thieves, and assorted members of organized crime. Not only did they associate with these undesirables, but they also helped them avoid arrest for the numerous robberies and burglaries they committed. In payment for their graft, they received a cut in all the cash and jewelry that was stolen.

In 1966, a Dade County grand jury returned indictments charging Manson Hill, Chief of Detectives, Sergeant Dave Hellman, head of the intelligence unit, and jewel thief Joseph Cacciatore, with an assortment of crimes. Cacciatore was the first cousin of Mafia crime boss, Santo Trafficante. He was also one of the notorious "Silk Stocking Bandits" who terrorized victims during armed home invasion robberies throughout Dade County.

One of the victims who testified against the trio was Mrs. Edwin Hydeman. She had a priceless gold bracelet stolen during a robbery. She told the grand jury that she was at Tropical Park racetrack in the grandstands one day when she saw a woman wearing her stolen bracelet. She called the police who confronted the woman. The woman identified herself as Mrs. Manson Hill, the wife of the Chief of Detectives at the Sheriff's Office.

The citizens of Dade County were infuriated by what the grand jury had uncovered. They demanded accountability. For decades, the Sheriff's Office had been rife with impropriety, and they wanted change. During the next election (1966), the voters abolished the office of the Sheriff and established the Director of Public Safety position.

E. Wilson Purdy was appointed the first Director of the newly formed Public Safety Department. Purdy was a former Military

Police Captain in the Army, and an FBI agent. He was notably straight arrow, no nonsense, and totally incorruptible. His leadership reformed the entire culture of the department. A devout Christian Scientist, who neither smoked nor drank, he identified those who were dishonest and fired them.

For the next 14 years, Director Purdy transformed the Metro-Dade Police Department into one of the finest police agencies in the country, and it remains so today. His legacy of professionalism and excellence at the Miami-Dade Police Department is undeniable.[43][44]

[43] From courtroom testimony and interviews conducted by Sgt. Dave Simmons and Det. Mike Hernandez.
[44] NEIA newsletter, misconduct, corruption and abuse of power, Edward J. Tully, May 1998.

ARRESTED: Marvin Baker is a 16-year police department veteran.

Figure 26. Disgraced Miami-Dade police officer Marvin Baker.

CHAPTER 11
The Twins

February 23, 1998,
2:30 p.m.

Exactly two weeks after the double murder at the Amoco gas station where Tyrone Tarver and Roger Davis were brutally mowed down with AK-47s, the Boobie Boys struck again. Two gunmen killed 30-year-old, John Davis, and wounded an innocent bystander at the 79th Street "One Stop" store. Davis was targeted because he was selling on Boobies's turf.

Boobie and Israel Baptiste had been squabbling for months over what Boobie called his "million-dollar hole" because of the high-traffic strip club located across the street. Boobie paid the owner of the store a small percentage of his sales for the rights to the parking lot. Baptiste refused to remove his people, so Boobie ordered the Twins, (Bo and Nard Brown), to take their territory back. Baptiste was the intended victim, but he was not there that day.

Davis was selling packets of crack when the Twins snuck up behind him and opened fire with .40 caliber pistols. Davis was hit multiple times and died instantly. The entire murder was caught on the store's video camera footage. Video technology was not as advanced in 1998 as it is today but, although it is blurry, it does accurately depict the crime. Corey Mucherson (AKA Fish Grease) was the getaway driver.

The death of John Davis convinced all of us on the newly formed North End Task Force just how crucial it was that we act quickly to end the violence. We needed to get the main players off the streets to stop the slaughter.

Our proposed strategy of securing warrants for federal gun violations was working even better than we had hoped. Detectives Jeff Lewis, Mike Hernandez, Chuck Clark, Joe Malott, and I scoured the criminal histories of the main players in both factions. We found numerous weapons charges that the Miami-Dade

State Attorney's Office had simply abandoned with no explanation.

Vonda Jackson, for example, was arrested on two separate occasions with a handgun in her possession. She was charged with carrying a concealed firearm and possession of a firearm by a convicted felon by the arresting officers in both cases. And in both cases, the charges were nolle prossed. That is, dropped, not dismissed by a judge, but inexplicably not prosecuted by the State Attorney's Office.

The more research we conducted, the angrier we got. Virtually every member of the Boobie Boys and Vonda's Gang had similar cases that were dumped by the Miami-Dade prosecutors. Cases that, if pursued, could have put these violent predators in prison and stopped some of the pointless killings. It was unfathomable.

The two federal agents assigned to the task force, Carlos Canino from ATF, and Lenny Athas from DEA, were a perfect fit. They had the same "let's put these assholes in prison" attitude that the rest of us did.

Agent Canino reviewed all the gun charges we submitted and presented them to AUSA Chris Clark to be filed. In most instances, the guns were still impounded and available as evidence. Carlos retrieved all the weapons and had them test fired at the Miami-Dade crime lab to see if they ballistically matched any of the murders. In several cases we hit the jackpot, and the lab made a match to the open homicides. Things were definitely falling into place quickly.

One day in mid-March, Lieutenant White called me into his office and said, "Dave Simmons from Northside District is being assigned to your task force. He'll start on Monday."

Sergeant Dave "Spiffy" Simmons had been a homicide detective in the 70s and early 80s. He worked on many high-profile cases, including serial killer Robert Frederick Carr. Carr was a pedophile who raped and strangled two 11-year-old boys who were reported missing while hitch hiking in North Miami Beach. He committed similar murders in Connecticut and Mississippi and was thought to have sexually molested hundreds of children.

Miami Herald reporter Edna Buchanan conducted over 120 hours of jail house interviews with Carr and authored a book that chronicled his crimes. When Carr died in a North Florida prison in 2007, Buchanan was quoted as saying, "He was about the most evil person I ever met. It's such good news that he is no longer on the planet."

Dave was given the nickname "Spiffy" early in his career because he looked like he stepped out of the pages of *GQ* magazine. He was always impeccably dressed in expensive three-piece suits that were a stark contrast to the suits I wore right off the rack from J. C. Penney's. We often joked that Dave probably slept in a suit. He was not only meticulous in his attire, but he was also an equally meticulous investigator. Every task force needs an "organizer" to keep track of everything, and Dave became ours.

While we were compiling the gun cases,

we began gathering information on both groups. I reached out to Detective Rodney Polite who first gave me Boobie's name during the Gerry Dukes murder investigation four years earlier. He put me in touch with several people who grew up with Boobie and knew him well.

Jeff Lewis had a huge stable of informants in the Carol City area, and he started contacting them one by one. From all these sources, we were able to identify many of the main players and put together rosters for both groups. A veritable Who's Who of criminals. But it was Chuck Clark who would discover the GOAT (greatest of all time) snitch.

One day in March, Chuck stuck his head in my cubicle. "Sarge, I just got a call from a guy who claims to know everything about the Boobie Boys. He wants to meet in the parking lot behind the library. You want to go?"

"Absolutely," I said as I grabbed my Beretta 9mm from the bottom drawer of my desk and holstered it. I snatched my hand-held radio out of the charger and headed out the door of the Homicide Office with Chuck.

When we pulled into the parking lot on the east side of the Carol City Public Library, we spotted a lone Black male seated on a bench. He waved us over and quickly climbed into the back seat of our car. He introduced himself as "Rodrick" and said, "Let's get out of here, so no one will see me with you guys."

For the next four hours, as we drove around Carol City, he filled us in on the hierarchy of the Boobie Boys and the criminal activities they were involved in. As he talked, I furiously scribbled page after page of notes on my yellow legal pad. He had grown up with Boobie and his inner circle and was still tight with all of them. As he talked, he gave Chuck directions and took us by the houses of the main players. He pointed out their girlfriends' houses as well.

Even though our county rental car had dark tinted windows, Rodrick was initially hesitant to point out the locations until we used an old Robbery Bureau trick. We stopped at a Publix Super Market, and I ran in and got an ordinary brown paper bag. I tore eyeholes in the bag and told Rodrick to put it over his head.

When we were in Robbery, we would use the paper bag over the head ploy to drive informants directly into the projects where they would point out the robbers they knew. We would often have a crowd around our car peering into the windows trying to figure out who the "unknown snitch" was.

Now feeling more comfortable with the bag, Rodrick agreed to take us to the favorite hangouts of the Boobie Boys. When he took us by the One-Of-a-Kind Bar, he pointed to two men standing near the front door.

"There go Boobie and E-4 right there," he said. That was the first time I had ever laid eyes on Kenneth "Boobie" Williams or Efrain "E-4" Casado.

Over the next three years, Rodrick remained a valuable source of information on the Boobie Boys. His tips were always on the money and led to the seizure of many automatic weapons and multiple kilos of cocaine. One day, he called the Homicide Office and said that two out of town dope dealers had just purchased three kilos of cocaine in Carol City. He added that they had boarded a Greyhound bus with a suitcase containing the three kilos and $280,000 in cash. The bus was bound for New York.

Jeff Lewis notified the Florida Highway Patrol who stopped the bus on I-95. Sure enough, in the baggage compartment of the Greyhound, a drug dog alerted on a light brown suitcase. When it was opened, it contained three kilos and $280,000. Half a million dollars in today's money.

As we dropped him off that first day, I asked Rodrick why he was helping us. "I thought you might throw some money my way sometimes," he said. "And besides, I get in trouble a lot, and I thought maybe you could help me out when I do." He gave us a slight smile and turned and walked away.

When I first came on the job, police

informers were known as "finks" on the street. I recall driving down 27th Avenue in 1974 and seeing, "FAT BRIGHT IS THE FINK" spray painted in gigantic letters on a wall. The day after the revelation appeared, Fat Bright was shot and killed in the parking lot of the Palace Bar. Whether the accusation was true or not, no one knows. But someone must have believed it.

Over time, "fink" was often broadened to "rat fink" as the preferred street lingo, and then simply "rat." "Snitch" emerged as a derogatory reference to police collaborators, sometime in the early 80s, I believe. The message outing Fat Bright remained emblazoned on that wall for years after his demise, probably as a warning to future finks.

By the end of April, we had identified twenty firearms cases that could be filed federally on members of both gangs. Chris Clark reviewed them and signed the complaints as quickly as he could.

One of the cases involved a vehicle chase in 1997 in the City of Miami. Boobie, E-4, and James "Vinnie" Deleveaux, fled from uniformed officers in a Honda that was reported stolen. During the pursuit, the occupants threw out two AK-47s, an Uzi sub machine-gun, bullet-proof vests, and ski masks. The trio bailed out of the SUV and fled on foot into a residential neighborhood. A perimeter was established, and a K-9 quickly located all three. They were all arrested and charged as felons in possession of firearms, but the State Attorney's Office, not surprisingly, declined to prosecute them.

Rodrick, our new CI, knew all about the incident. He said they had received information that Vonda was hosting a party in Overtown. They knew Rah-Rah and the rest of her crew would be there, and they were on their way to kill them all when the police intervened.

By the beginning of May, we had active federal warrants for all the main players and even some of the lesser participants. The federal firearms statute was a great tool to swiftly dismantle the two gangs.

The penalties were harsh, and the elements were easy to prove. The law doesn't even require the possession of a gun. Possession of ammunition violates the statute equally. A career criminal caught with a single bullet in his pants pocket could conceivably go to federal prison for 20 years. The adage often repeated on the streets is, "The Feds don't play."

The first of either crew to be arrested was Famous Johnson. The MDPD Career Criminal Unit located him and brought him to the Homicide Office where I interviewed him. He was young, arrogant, and cocky. He was convinced that the gun charges would be dropped just like they always had been and refused to talk about his relationship with Vonda. I guess no one told him "the Feds don't play."

He did, however, want to talk about the murder of his close friend, Roger Davis, who was killed two months earlier at the Amoco gas station. He claimed that Johnathon Hawthorne (AKA Moose) was there when the murder occurred. He said that Moose was not one of the shooters but possibly drove the getaway car. He maintained that the murders were payback for Moose being shot a year earlier in Overtown.

Famous told Jeff Lewis, the lead detective on the Roger Davis case, that Moose cut his hair the day after the murder because news reports maintained that one of the attackers had long dreadlocks. Jeff was able to locate a jail booking photo taken six days before the murder that showed Moose with long dreadlocks. He also found a booking photo taken ten days after the murder that depicted Moose with a shaved head.

I checked the name Johnathon Hawthorne in the criminal computer system and found that he had an open warrant for violation of probation. He also had a court date in 72 hours on an unrelated matter.

I sat in the courtroom three days later not sure if he would show up or not. But he did, and as he walked out of the courtroom, I arrested him. Back at the

Homicide Office, he was eager to talk about himself being shot, but denied any involvement in the murder of Roger Davis.

He said, in 1995, he opened a drug hole in Overtown that directly conflicted with an operation already in place and controlled by Vonda Jackson. When Eddie Donaldson was murdered along with two others on the Palmetto Expressway, Moose decided to take over his "spot." Using $750 he won in a Bolita game, he bought some crack and began selling. He assumed that since Donaldson was dead anyone could take over his location.

Apparently, Vonda disagreed and sent Rah-Rah and Famous to kill him. Both were armed with AK-47s. He was shot multiple times in an ambush in front of his father's house. He remained on the verge of death for months in the ICU at Jackson Hospital. He was paralyzed from the waist down as a result of the attack and was treated at the Miami Project to Cure Paralysis for a year until he was able to walk again. All at taxpayer expense. This was the first time he told any police officer or detective who shot him.

Several days later, Jeff Lewis and I signed Mario Frazier out of the Miami-Dade County Stockade and brought him to the Homicide Office. He was at the stockade awaiting trial on theft charges. Jeff took a sworn statement from him regarding the triple murder he witnessed on the Palmetto Expressway in which E-4 and Boobie shot and killed three members of Vonda's Gang. The lead detective on that case, Juan Capote, was out of state on an investigative trip and asked that the statement be taken.

While talking to Frazier, we also discovered that he and his mother were eyewitness to the double murder at the Amoco gas station. He positively identified E-4 from photos as one of the participants. Later that day, Jeff located Frazier's mother who corroborated her son's story and also positively identified E-4 from a photo lineup.

In late March, I learned that detectives

from the Warrants Bureau had arrested Vonda Jackson. She had been booked into the Women's Detention Center on 7th Avenue and was awaiting transfer to the Federal Detention Center by the U. S. Marshalls.

I talked to Vonda at length that evening. She was cordial but cagey. She agreed to talk to me but was very careful with her answers. I took ten pages of notes on a legal pad, but very little of it was useful. What I did accomplish, however, was to get her to admit that she knew all the players. This would be helpful for the impending Federal CCE case.

Vonda did reveal a couple of tidbits. She said that when her three "friends" were shot and killed on the Palmetto Expressway, the lone survivor, Andre McWhorter (AKA Bam), saw the killers without their masks. Bam said he played dead when Boobie and E-4 came to the car to "finish them off." He said he saw their faces clearly but did not tell the police.

Vonda also talked a little about the docks and how easy it was to smuggle narcotics into the Port. She said she and her whole family were longshoremen, and her father, who was head of the longshoreman's union, was about to retire. She explained that any successful smuggling operation required the complicity of a gantry operator. A gantry is a crane that is used to move sealed shipping containers. If a container contains kilos of cocaine, the gantry operator can move it to avoid inspection by U. S. Customs Agents or place it in a hidden area where the narcotics can be secretly unloaded.

Vonda said that just recently a gantry operator named, Lionel Porter, had stolen 80 kilos from a shipment. The Colombian who the kilos were meant for came to Lionel's house in Carol City and put a gun in his mother's mouth threatening to "blow her brains out of the top of her head." Lionel returned the 80 kilos.

Vonda also told me Moose was at the *Amoco* murders, and that he cut his dreadlocks off the next day because of the news reports. According to Vonda, the Twins were calling Moose "soft and a coward" because he didn't seek revenge after he was shot. The Twins were relentless with their abuse, calling him "soft as cotton" and a "pussy," so he agreed to participate in the *Amoco* murders "to show he had heart." Vonda did admit to me that it was Rah-Rah and Famous who shot Moose, but she would not concede that she ordered the "hit".

The next to go down was E-4. He was arrested by MDPD detectives and ATF agents who pounced on him as he left his house. He was charged with Federal firearms violations stemming from the chase in the city in which several weapons were ejected from the vehicle. He was brought to the Homicide Office and interviewed by Jeff and DEA agent Lenny Athas but refused to talk without a lawyer.

He did agree to provide background about himself though. He said he dropped out of Miami Central High School in the 10th grade and in 1989, married Keytrona Johnson. They had four children together: Nyima (age 5), Nyisha (age 4), Efrain, Jr.

(age 3), and Eprain (age 2). He stated that his only source of income was a lawn cutting business called E&D Landscaping.

Jeff noticed that E-4 was covered with numerous tattoos on his arms, legs, chest and back, so he summoned a crime scene tech to take close-up color photographs of them. An elaborate tattoo covered his entire back that portrayed an open bible emblazoned with two bible verses:

Isaiah 54:17
No weapon that is formed against thee shall prosper; and every tongue that shall rise against thee in judgment thou shalt condemn. This is the heritage of the servants of the LORD, and their righteousness is of me, saith the LORD.

Psalm 4:1-8
Hear me when I call, O God of my righteousness: Thou hast enlarged me when I was in distress; Have mercy upon me and hear my prayer. O ye sons of men, how long will ye turn my glory into shame?

It was a magnificent piece of artwork,

intricate and ornate. Just above the Bible was the face of Jesus wearing a crown of thorns. It revealed a complete dichotomy between E-4's gangster lifestyle and his Catholic upbringing.

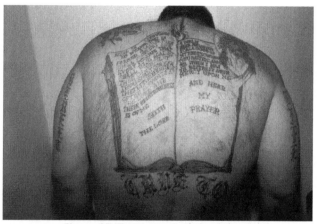

Figure 27. Tattoo on E-4's back (Author)

E-4 had $10,000 in cash in his pockets at the time of his arrest. A police K-9 alerted on the money as having cocaine residue on it and it was seized. It was later learned that the $10,000 was to be used as bond money for fellow Boobie Boy, Zeus Wilson, who had been jailed for selling cocaine. E-4 claimed he won the money gambling, and it was to be used to pay off his home mortgage.

Three days later E-4 was charged with assaulting one of the corrections officers at the Federal Detention Center. Cheryl Palmer, an investigator for the Bureau of Prisons asked me to come to her office where she showed me a video tape of E-4 punching and kicking one of the guards.

E-4 and two other prisoners had barricaded themselves into a cell, and when officers broke through the barricade and entered the cell, E-4 attacked them. As punishment, E-4 was sent to the Special Housing Unit known as the SHU (pronounced shoe) or "the hole."

The SHU is the lowest, worst possible existence in the federal prison system. The inmate is confined to a 7x9 cell with only a toilet, sink and bunk. All privileges are taken away or severely cut back. TV, radio, and books are not allowed. Meals are served on a tray that is pushed through a slot in the steel door. There is no communication with other prisoners. It is a miserable punishment, and most inmates don't do well mentally in the SHU.

While there, I asked Cheryl if I could look at E-4's file. In it I discovered a lot of material that would be useful in the upcoming CCE. During questioning by booking officers, E-4 admitted his close association with Boobie and insisted that he be kept separate from any member of Vonda's crew. The booking officer wrote down his exact words: *"I'm a member of the Boobie Boys gang. We're at war with Vonda's gang. Vonda's people have tried to kill me seven times. I need to be kept away from Vonda's people."*

Figure 28. Efrain Casado, AKA E-4. (Author)

Shortly after E-4's arrest, Mike

Hernandez and I picked up our new CI, Rodrick, and brought him to the Homicide Office. We showed him the video that captured the murder of John Davis at the 79th Street "One Stop" store. Without hesitating, he said, "That's the Twins. Bo and Nard." He also told us that Nard had a severe heart condition requiring that he go to Jackson Memorial Hospital once a month, every month, and receive a life-sustaining shot.

The North End Task Force had been in existence for less than three months and we had already been able to arrest or secure arrest warrants for the most vicious members in each criminal organization. Boobie and Rah-Rah were wanted for federal firearms violations. E-4, Vonda and Famous Johnson were in custody. And the Twins, Bo and Nard Brown, had been indicted for first degree murder. Overall, we were pleased with our initial results, but there was still more work to be done.

CHAPTER TWELVE
Fish Grease

I was immersed in reviewing a suicide report one afternoon when Captain Butler wandered into my cubicle and sat on the corner of my desk.

"The third floor wants you to give Gail Epstein from the *Miami Herald* an interview about the Boobie Boys case," he said without any preamble.

I was stunned. I tossed my pen onto my desk and said, "Captain, just two months ago, we had a sergeant's meeting where we were told not to talk to Gail Epstein under any circumstances. We were told she was not to be trusted and to always refer her to PIO (the public information office). Never talk to her, the lieutenant said."

He nodded his head vigorously. "I know. I know. I know. But things have apparently changed. She has the Director's ear now, and he wants her to have full access to any information about this gang war."

"Captain, this is a really bad idea," I

said. "It's going to hurt our investigation by publicizing what we're doing."

"I agree, but it's been decided."

"Okay," I said. "But this is not going to be good."

I couldn't have been more wrong.

Two days later, I sat in the homicide conference room with Gail Epstein and showed her the same slide presentation I had given to the command staff in February. I was amazed by how much she already knew. She had been conducting her own investigation and interviewing the family members of many of the homicide victims. I confirmed for her a lot of what she had already uncovered.

Her article was published in the Sunday edition of the *Herald* on Mother's Day, May 10th, 1998, and it was a blockbuster. It took up two complete pages and gave every sordid detail of the conflict between the two groups. When the morning edition hit the street, the article caused a huge furor in Overtown, Carol City and the rest of Miami-Dade County. After the word spread, the first printing sold out in minutes. The *Herald* press room rushed out two more printings to keep up with the demand, but they sold out just as quickly. People were driving as far as Palm Beach County and Homestead to buy copies.

The headline read "Deadly Gang Wars" in large red letters. The front page showed color photos of Boobie, Vonda, E-4, Rah-Rah, The Twins, Marvin Rogers, Zeus, and Famous Johnson. There was also a map showing the location of the murders and shootings. It was quite impressive.

The first eight paragraphs set the tone of the article:

With deadly regularity, dueling drug-traffickers outfitted with AK-47s are marking their territory with indiscriminate barrages of unstoppable firepower. As many as 100 shootings appear to be linked to a handful of warring drug factions in Miami-Dade, police say.

Take or be taken. It's the law of the street.

It's also the credo that has turned the drive-by shooting into a horrific art form in Miami-

Dade's poorest inner-city neighborhoods.

But now the hammer is dropping. In surgical strikes that started two weeks ago, police and prosecutors are using federal firearms indictments in an attempt to dismantle the leadership ranks of Miami-Dade's most violent drug gangs. Convictions would mean long federal prison sentences and the promise of serious charges, including murder, down the road.

The foremost goal: saving lives.

"We've had an artificially inflated murder rate as these guys shot it out," said Frank Boni, assistant chief for Miami-Dade Police. "I think now the murder rate will drop off."

"That prediction will be welcome news to thousands of beleaguered inner-city residents routinely forced to duck and dive from gunfire," said State Representative Kendrick Meek, who had pushed police to reclaim every hostile street.

"These guys are selling drugs...it's their kingdom," Meek said during a recent tour of Liberty City's worst drug holes. "You've got 1 per cent of the people holding the rest of the community hostage. And they are brutal! AK-47s, 9mm's. The casualties are in the drug

trade, but innocent people die, too."

Further down in the article, Epstein explained our strategy:

The U.S. Attorney's Office agreed to file firearms charges under federal law. Both alleged gang leaders were indicted in April along with three of their alleged lieutenants. Police arrested Vonda Jackson, but Boobie Williams is believed to have fled the state and is still being sought.

On conviction, the firearms charge carries a minimum-mandatory sentence of 10 years. It can be made even longer for violent career criminals.

The article ended with the tease: Coming Monday. The families affected by the gang violence.

The article turned out to be a bombshell. It ignited a firestorm in South Florida. As soon as the first edition hit the streets on Mother's Day the phone in the Homicide Office began ringing off the hook. The three homicide detectives who were working were deluged with calls from people who professed to have information about both groups. One of them called me at home. "You need to get in here with your squad right away, Sarge," he said. "We can't handle all these calls."

And it didn't stop. The volume of calls decreased over time, but for the next two years, we continued to receive call after call from witnesses willing to help. Many of them were inmates, or the family members of inmates, who wanted their sentences reduced through cooperation. Dozens of family members in Miami clipped out the *Miami Herald* article and mailed it to their relatives imprisoned in federal facilities. Inmates from south Florida passed it around on the yard to other inmates. We were soon getting hundreds of calls and letters from convicts willing to testify against the Boobie Boys or Vonda's Gang.

Why would anyone in federal prison jeopardize being labeled a snitch, agree to testify in open court, and risk retaliation from other prisoners you might ask? The answer: a Rule 35.

Federal prison sentences are known to be severe. Harsh in fact. Thirty-to-forty-year stretches (even life sentences) for trafficking in narcotics are common. According to the guidelines:

• A person commits the crime of federal drug trafficking when he or she manufactures, distributes, dispenses, or possesses with intent to manufacture, distribute, or dispense *any* amount of a prohibited controlled substance.

• The U.S. sentencing guidelines considers three primary factors in drug crimes: whether the offense harmed another person; whether there was a weapon involved; and the criminal history of the defendant.

• Any person involved in the importation or exportation of controlled substances is subject to a penalty of 5, 10, or 20 years, or even life imprisonment, with fines starting at $2 million and can reach as high as $20 million.

- Federal drug or violent crimes involving the use of a firearm require stiff mandatory minimum sentencing, with 5 to 10 years being added to the underlying offense when the defendant is a first offender and 25 years when the defendant is a second offender. If the firearm is a machine gun or destructive device and the firearm is equipped with a silencer, 30 years is added to the underlying offense, and if the defendant is a second offender, a life sentence is added.

Eighty percent of all federal defendants facing a mandatory minimum sentence stand convicted of a drug crime. A mandatory minimum sentence for a federal drug crime imposes a binding prison term for no less than a specific period of time. That is, no parole and no early release for "good behavior."

In the state courts, federal trafficking would be considered mere possession. With the Feds it can be life altering. When convicted federally, most people are shocked to learn just how crushing the sentencing guidelines are. For many, their only hope of ever seeing freedom again is a Rule 35.

The Federal Rule of Criminal Procedure 35(b) allows offenders who cooperate with the government to receive credit for the "substantial assistance" they provide in the arrest and prosecution of another person. Generally, a request must be filed within one year of sentencing, BUT if the defendant could not have "reasonably anticipated" that the information in question would be useful until more than a year after sentencing, the one-year requirement is waived. If the prosecuting United States Attorney and the sentencing judge agree that the assistance the defendant has given is substantial, the defendant's sentence may be reduced.

On the outside these criminals would vow to each other that they would never "rat." That they would be "soldiers, true to the streets, and true to the game." But once they were inside, it was a different story. Faced with the prospect of dying in prison, they all agreed to "spill their guts." There were so many in federal prison who were cooperating with authorities that informers were no longer stigmatized or attacked.

The story in the *Miami Herald* and the Federal Rule 35 undeniably changed the entire direction of our investigation. While we were previously scrounging for witnesses and begging them to come forward, we now had more witnesses than we could handle.

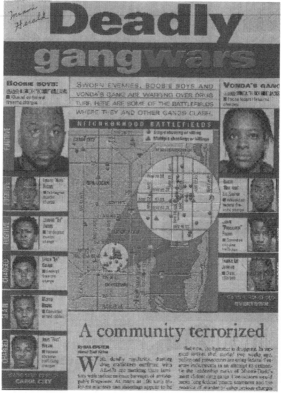

Figure 29. The above article was published in the Miami Herald on Mother's Day 1998. (Miami Herald).

On May 11th, the day after Gail Epstein's story appeared in the Miami Herald newspaper, Corey Mucherson, who was also known as "Fish Grease," was murdered in Titusville, a small town two hundred miles north of Miami.

Joe Malott spoke to his cousin Kimberly

Cohen the next day. She said that just before Fish Grease was killed, he had read the article about the Miami gang violence in the Sunday edition of the *Herald*. After reading it, he seemed visibly upset, and his cousin asked him what was wrong. He said simply, "There's a bunch of mess going on in Miami. I made my bed, and now I gotta lay in it."

A few minutes later, he walked out of the front door of her apartment and was gunned down. He was shot multiple times by a gunman dressed in dark clothing and wearing a nylon stocking as a mask. Fish Grease had only arrived at the apartment a few hours earlier so his cousin speculated that he must have been followed.

Services for Fish Grease were held in Miami at the Brownsville Baptist Church on the following Saturday. At the funeral, several family members were overheard angrily accusing Boobie and the Twins of complicity in Fish Grease's death. Overcome with grief, they loudly proclaimed that Boobie considered Fish Grease a "weak link" and that he was murdered by Boobie to "shut him up." They even alleged that following the murder, Boobie and the Twins went to nearby Disney World and were spotted there by friends of the Mucherson family. This was reported to us months later by informants, but none of the family ever voiced their suspicions to the Titusville police.

Fish Grease and Boobie had been friends since elementary school. When Boobie rose to power and took over the Matchbox projects, Fish Grease was right by his side. He was a loyal follower of Boobie for over a decade. But those who knew him said there was no doubt that, for his own self-preservation, Boobie would not hesitate to do away with one of his closest homeboys if he thought it was necessary.

Fish Grease's murder has never been solved.

CHAPTER 13
Death

One week after the *Herald* article was published, I received a phone call from Assistant United States Attorney Fernando Groene from the Eastern District of Virginia in Norfolk. He said that he was in the process of putting together a continuing criminal enterprise (CCE) case regarding Richard Thomas Stitt (AKA: DEATH).

Stitt, as you will recall, was one of the suspected shooters in the double homicide at the Amoco gas station. He and his girlfriend also rented the getaway vehicle using the alias, Errol Joseph.

Groene said that he was preparing to indict at least a dozen defendants, charging them with numerous violations of federal narcotics and firearms laws and drug-related murders. His plan was to include eight murders in the CCE that occurred in the Norfolk/Portsmouth area. He went on to say that he currently had enough evidence and testimony to include Boobie and many of his cohorts in the indictment.

One of those he intended to add was Jason Ortega, a close associate of Boobie's. He planned to charge Ortega with at least three murders. He aimed to seek the death penalty for both Stitt and Ortega. In discussions he had with Ortega's attorney, he was confident that Ortega would agree to testify against Stitt if he were indicted to avoid the death penalty.

Groene said he anticipated presenting the case to the grand jury within the next 30 days but would like to meet with the North End Task Force and AUSA Chris Clark before he did. I told him we were putting together a similar CCE case on the Boobie Boys and he said, "I don't want to step on your toes down there. If you have enough to charge Boobie and his people, it would make more sense to indict them in Miami. I have enough on my plate right now with defendants who are from Virginia."

Before we hung up, Groene agreed to fly to Miami and meet with the Task Force to share information and hammer out a strategy. He said he would bring his two lead investigators, Detective Tammy Early from the Portsmouth Police Department and Special Agent Hugh Ruegsegger of the FBI.

One week later, I picked up the three of them at Miami International Airport and drove them to the Homicide Office. We spent the next two days in the conference room brainstorming and dividing the cases. We all got along great. There was no bickering or any territorial disputes. Our goal was to put as many of these thugs in federal prison, for the rest of their lives, as we could.

AUSA Groene was particularly interested in the double murder at the Amoco gas station because of the similarities to one of the cases he intended to include in his CCE. In the Virginia murder, a stolen car was used and dumped a block away. There the killers got into a vehicle rented by Stitt's girlfriend, Tanaka Stringer, just like in the Amoco murders. Because of the similarities, Groene immediately issued a grand jury subpoena for Tanaka Stringer who rented the vehicle used in the Amoco case. He asked that members of the North End Task Force locate Stringer and serve her with the subpoena.

Two weeks later, AUSA Greone called and told me that he had secured the indictments. As expected, Jason Ortega quickly pleaded guilty and agreed to testify against Stitt (Death) and all the others named in the CCE.

During a debriefing with the FBI, Ortega told them that he and Stitt had worked directly for Boobie and Darrell Green in their Virginia operation since the early 90s. He went on to say that Darrell Green had recently been convicted in Pensacola by the DEA and was serving a life sentence in federal prison.

He also revealed some stunning new information. From prison, Death (Richard Stitt) was conspiring to have witnesses against him killed. Right after they were arrested, they were in the same lock up for several days, and Stitt told Ortega, "Hang tight. Boobie is going to clean this up for us. They won't be any witnesses left to testify." He told Ortega that he had to be "stand up" and that if anyone came forward against them, Boobie would have their families killed. He said confidently, "Boobie can reach out and get anyone."

Stitt said that Boobie still had "shooters out there who would take care of business" Two names he specifically mentioned were Linard Albury (AKA Shotout) and Shauntell Seay (AKA Red Boy). According to Stitt, both were fanatically loyal to Boobie and would do anything he asked, including kill witnesses.

Ortega also revealed that, for the past year, Stitt knew he was being investigated. In August of 1997, he summoned Jason Ortega and Jason Davis to a meeting at the Majik City Go-Go Bar where he ordered them to assassinate Detective Tammy Early and Detective Michael Holley of the Portsmouth Police Department. In addition, he wanted FBI Special Agent Thomas Blades killed. He indicated that he was trying to find out the name of the U. S. Attorney in charge of the case and that when he did, he said, "I want him dead, too."

Stitt went on to tell Ortega that he was aware of the investigation because several deputies he knew, and had paid off in the jail, were present when Early, Holley, and Blades talked to prisoners about him. He provided Ortega with the home addresses of Detectives Early and Holley and FBI agent Blades. Stitt obtained the addresses from contacts he had in the DMV.

During the de-briefing, Ortega recalled that Detective Holley lived in Portsmouth on Elmhurst Lane and that Detective Early lived in Chesapeake, but he couldn't recall her address. Ortega said that he and Davis fully intended to carry out the "hits" but were arrested before they could do so. He and Davis spent many hours surveilling both Holley and Early, looking for an opportune moment to kill them. They knew, for example, that Holley lived near Hardee's restaurant and would buy his coffee there every morning. They planned to do a drive-by shooting while he was at the drive-up window.

Shortly after Ortega and Stitt were arrested, they were in a U. S. Marshal's van being transported to the Federal Courthouse for a hearing when Stitt told Ortega that he now knew the prosecutor's name, Fernando Groene. He said he was going to arrange to have Groene killed. One of their co-defendants riding in the van, Kermit Brown, spoke up and said, "That won't do you no good, man. They just put another one in his place. They got hundreds of them."

Death slowly nodded his head and said, "Yeah, you may be right."

The trial lasted for two months. In the end, all eight defendants were found guilty by a 12-member jury. After the trial, AUSA Groene subpoenaed Jeff Lewis and I to testify at the death sentencing hearing for Stitt. He wanted us to tell the jury about the Amoco gas station double murder and about the Boobie Boys organization in general.

We flew to Norfolk, and we each testified for over four hours. At the hearing,

Stitt's defense attorneys presented what they called mitigating reasons why Stitt should not be executed which included:

-The victims consented to the criminal conduct that resulted in their deaths.

-The other factors in the defendant's background or character mitigate against the imposition of the death sentence.

-Richard Thomas Stitt was subjected to a dysfunctional family setting in childhood.

-Richard Thomas Stitt was abandoned and neglected as a child.

-Richard Thomas Stitt was deprived of the parental guidance and protection which he needed as a child.

-There are factors in Richard Thomas Stitt's background which demonstrate that mercy should be considered.

The hearing testimony lasted five days,

and the jury deliberated for three days, before unanimously recommending that Stitt be sentenced to death on each of the three counts of homicide.

Following the jury's recommendation, the district court sentenced Stitt to death on each of his three convictions for murder under the Federal Drug Kingpin statute. In addition, Stitt was sentenced to a total of 780 months (65 years) to be served consecutively for his two convictions of using and carrying a firearm during and in relation to a crime of violence and for his two convictions of using and carrying a firearm during and in relation to a drug trafficking crime.

Death was sentenced to death. How ironic.

Ortega did, in fact, testify against Stitt during the trial, and because of his cooperation, the Feds waived the death penalty. He was sentenced to life in prison plus 30 years. Further cooperation resulted in his release in 2020.

Following the death sentence, Stitt's

attorney, Norman Malinski, reached out to me with a proffer hoping for a Rule 35 for his client. He called Fernando Groene "a runaway prosecutor with no heart."

In the proffer, Stitt admitted his involvement in the murders of Tyrone Tarver and Roger Davis, at the *Amoco* gas station. He also claimed to know who killed Bennie Brownlee, Walter Betterson, Derrick Harris, and many others he said we didn't know about. He said he would testify against Boobie.

When I told prosecutor Chris Clark about the offer, his reply was, "Absolutely not. We are making no deals with admitted and convicted killers."

I agreed wholeheartedly.

Figure 30. Richard Stitt, AKA Death. (Author)

CHAPTER 14
Karen

"Nard" Brown was caught fleeing from the parking lot of Coco's Lounge, a strip club on NW 119th Street. Miami-Dade police officers were dispatched to a disturbance call, and he ran when they pulled up. He was found hiding behind a house in a nearby residential neighborhood and charged with resisting arrest. Three other men ran at the same time, and two handguns were dropped on the asphalt as they fled. Nard gave a false name when he was booked into the Miami-Dade County Jail, but his fingerprints connected him to the first-degree murder warrant for the shooting death of John Davis. His twin brother "Bo" Brown may have been one of those who fled and got away.

A short article about his apprehension appeared in the *Miami Herald*:

The Brown brothers are wanted in connection with the slaying of John Davis who was gunned down on February 24 outside a market on Northwest 79th Street.

Police said the Browns forced four people to the ground at gunpoint. Davis was killed and another man was wounded and a third was shot at but escaped injury.

Karen Mills-Francis, lawyer for the Browns, did not return phone messages. She has previously denied they were involved in the slaying of Davis.

Karen Mills-Francis was the Boobie Boys' lawyer, spokesperson, and denier-in-chief. Whenever anyone in the group was accused of any type of criminal activity, she would vociferously deny it. When the Mother's Day article came out in the *Miami Herald*, reporter Gail Epstein asked her about the gang, and her reply was typical:

Karen Mills-Francis, Lawyer for several alleged players in the Boobie Boys said she had never heard of the gang's name before a reporter asked her about it. "They are called the Boobie

Boys? Let me write that down." She said.

Mills-Francis denied that "Boobie" Williams heads a gang. She said her clients the Brown twins, "don't know anything about" the murder police are seeking them for. She complained the FBI is so eager to take down Williams that agents used "Gestapo tactics" against a former client of hers to try to force him into becoming a government witness.

Karen Mills-Francis was born and raised in Miami. The oldest of five children, she was valedictorian of her high school class and accepted a full scholarship to the prestigious Bowdoin College in Brunswick, Maine where she received her baccalaureate degree. She graduated from the Levin School of Law at the University of Florida in 1987 and began her legal career at the Miami-Dade County Public Defender's Office. Eventually she moved into private practice. She shared an office on Biscayne Boulevard with another defense attorney, Larry Handfield, who was a former prosecutor under Janet Reno.

In 2000, Karen Mills-Francis ran for judge. She beat the longtime incumbent becoming only the second black woman in history to serve on the bench in Miami-Dade County. She won another term, and in 2008, she resigned to accept the starring role in the television series, "*Judge Karen*."

A knock off of other court shows, such as *The People's Court* and *Judge Judy*, she presided over small claims court cases as an arbitrator and proclaimed at the start of each show, "Justice isn't always black or white." The show was produced by Sony Pictures Television and lasted only one season, but episodes can still be seen today on the BET Network. In 2009, Mills-Francis was featured in another court show called *Judge Karen's Court*.

Judge Karen's Court—like *Judge Karen*—was axed after one season. In 2013, Entertainment Studios agreed to produce *Supreme Justice with Judge Karen*, which became moderately successful and was still in production in 2021.

But the ascendancy of Karen Mills-Francis from defense attorney to judge to television personality was nearly derailed by her involvement with the Boobie Boys.

On July 1, 1998, a federal grand jury was impaneled to hear evidence exclusively for the CCE case pertaining to the Boobie Boys and Vonda's Gang. I was the first witness to testify. I laid out what we knew so far and what we hoped to achieve.

A federal grand jury consists of 16 to 23 members, randomly selected from a list of registered voters. The federal grand jury meets behind closed doors and conducts its business in secret. Violations of the grand jury secrecy rules are strict. There is no presiding judge. Only the jurors, the prosecutor, and the witnesses are allowed in the jury room. The defendant has no right to be present or to even be informed that he or she is the subject of an investigation. Refusal to testify in front of the grand jury can result in a contempt charge.

The North End Task Force had spent six months trying to decide which witnesses merited an appearance before the grand jury. We travelled to numerous federal prisons, including Atlanta, Lewisburg, Coleman, Allenwood, and Leavenworth penitentiaries, conducting interviews, trying to establish who were the strongest witnesses, and which ones to reject.

Eventually, the travel was curtailed, and the witnesses were brought to us. Chris Clark signed writs ordering the U. S. Marshalls Service to transport the prisoners who were potential witnesses to Miami.

The Marshalls have a unique method for preventing escape plots. It is known as "diesel therapy." The inmate is not given any notice that he will be travelling. He is simply told, "pack your shit" and put on a bus or plane and taken to another facility where he is temporarily housed for a day or days. He is then again told to "pack your shit" and taken to another facility. This can go on for weeks.

The process is intended to confuse the inmate and not allow him to plan an escape with any of his confederates on the outside. A trip to Miami, for example, might start in Atlanta with a flight to Minnesota, then to

Oklahoma, then to Indiana, then a bus ride to Illinois and finally a flight to Miami. The inmates hated it, and it would be the first thing they complained about whenever we interviewed them.

By the fall of 1998, the house of cards that was the Boobie Boys organization had completely collapsed. It had proven to be a flimsy structure built on the loyalty of its members and the tensile strength of that loyalty was unexpectedly weak. The same was true for Vonda's Gang. Both groups were in total disarray. We had more informers and cooperators than we knew what to do with. The Mother's Day article in the *Miami Herald* had been a boon to the investigation and produced collaborators for us, both on the streets and in the prisons, who were willing to talk.

Vonda, Famous Johnson, Vonda's sister Coco, Pookalotta, E-4, Chico, Shotout, Fat Wayne, Vinnie, and Moose were in custody on federal firearms and drug charges. Nard and Death had been arrested for murder. Fish Grease was dead, and Boobie and Bo

Brown were on the run. Not bad for a start.

One of the sources we relied on was a 20-year-old female named Nettie. She called the homicide office one day asking for me because my name was mentioned several times in the article in the *Herald*. She said she was one of Boobie's many girlfriends. She had three kids, and she "thought" Boobie might be the father of the youngest.

Nettie confided that Boobie was worried. He had read the indictments for E-4 and the Twins and told her, "The cops know too much. Somebody is working for the cops. I don't know how they know all of this. They know everything."

He went on to tell her that he had hired two "good" lawyers and that the first thing the lawyers said to him was, "This isn't going to be cheap. Can you afford us?"

He told Nettie he laughed in their faces and said, "Yeah, I can afford you." The attorneys then explained to him how to funnel money to them through friends and family members by making "a bunch of payments that would not raise any red flags."

He went on to tell her that he might try and run to Atlanta, and that he had already made arrangements for plastic surgery, but he knew that it was over. He acknowledged he would probably be going to jail for the rest of his life and said pensively, "If I could only kill Rah-Rah, I could go to jail happy."

When we received information that Robert Sawyer (Rah-Rah) had fled back to Tallahassee, I contacted a United States Marshall I knew named Harry Lane, who worked in the Florida panhandle. I told him we had open federal warrants for Rah-Rah and his wife Andrea for firearms violations.

Harry said he was very familiar with Rah-Rah. Just two weeks earlier, a man named Alexander Ray King (AKA Bama) had been shot and killed at the Moon Bar in Tallahassee on what was known as Urban Ladies Night. Bama owed money to Rah-Rah for narcotics and the shooter in the homicide was Henry Lee Dickey, a cousin of Rah-Rah's wife. The day after the murder, Rah-Rah threatened Bama's girlfriend, telling her that even though Bama was dead, the debt was still owed, and she would be killed if it wasn't paid. Within a few days, Harry called to tell me that both Rah-Rah and his wife were in custody in Macon, Georgia.

All of us on the task force assumed that Rah-Rah would be "hardcore" and never talk to us. He had a reputation as a "stand-up guy" because he did his ten-year stretch for the contract killing of McBride without implicating Vonda. But this was different. He knew this was bad. He was facing life in prison. He had his ear to the street, and he knew other people were talking. So, two days after his arrest, he contacted his lawyer and told him he wanted to make a deal.

An agreement was hammered out quickly with his attorney, Clyde Taylor. Rah-Rah said he wanted to tell his side of the story. Yes, he had done some bad things, but the Boobie Boys were always trying to kill him. Sergeant Dave Simmons and Detective Mike Hernandez flew to Macon to hear his version.

It took a while for him to get on board, but when he did, he was all in, and he admitted to most of what he had done. He was reluctant to discuss the murders, particularly that of Marvin Rogers, but he did indicate that if his wife were released on bond, she "might" know the location of the murder weapon.

Dave and Mike took several sworn taped statements from Rah-Rah in which he fully admitted his participation with Vonda in the narcotics business. He also gave detailed statements describing how he had been shot multiple times by the Boobie Boys. For the first time in his life, he was willing to identify his attackers and prosecute them.

Mike Solis, the Assistant United States Attorney prosecuting the Sawyers, was accommodating. He agreed to ask for a low bond for Andrea Sawyer, and true to his word, Rah-Rah instructed her to turn over the H&K .223 rifle that was used to kill Marvin Rogers. (Ballistics testing would later confirm that it was one of the murder weapons).

We couldn't find Boobie or his cousin Bo Brown, so I called Cindy Smith, one of the producers at *America's Most Wanted*, the television show hosted by John Walsh. She agreed to produce a segment to try and help us capture them. The episode aired on Saturday night September 26, 1998, and was narrated by John Turchin. It was an exceptionally well-done piece and accurately depicted the drug war that had been raging on the streets of Miami for nearly a decade.

Detective Joe Malott flew to Washington, D.C. where the show originated and represented the task force as it was broadcast live. Joe helped man the tip line during and after the show.

An anonymous call came in that claimed Bo Brown was hiding out in the panhandle, in Gretna, Florida, where he had family. According to the tipster, Bo's father, known only as Top Cat, lived there, and was concealing him. Joe called the Gadsden

County Sheriff's Office in Quincy, and within hours Bo was in handcuffs. He had a .32 caliber pistol and $2500 in cash with him when he was arrested.

A receipt found in the Chevy Impala Bo was driving indicated he had purchased $250 worth of rap CDs from a store the day before. When Gadsden County detectives talked to the clerk, she identified pictures of both Bo and Boobie, and said they were in the store together.

An article in the *Miami Herald* the next day said, *"the arrest was another victory for law enforcement officers trying to bring down the Boobie Boys and Vonda's Gang, two violent drug organizations battling for control of Miami's drug market."*

Figure 31. Leonard "Bo" Brown. (Author)

Now that both of the twins, Bo and Nard, were finally in custody, the murder case against them could proceed. After three days of testimony from four eyewitnesses, the jury deliberated just over two hours and returned verdicts of not guilty on all six counts. It was a shocker, but we soon found out why there had been an acquittal.

In a *Miami Herald* article, Karen Mills-Francis, their attorney, said, "They were falsely accused, which is what I have always said from the beginning."

In her closing argument Mills-Francis attacked the prosecution witnesses as "gypsies, tramps, and thieves" who were more interested in cutting their own deals than in telling the truth. But as it turned out, she was apparently the unscrupulous one. A key witness at the trial alleged that Mill-Francis paid him to change his testimony. In a deposition, his entire story changed, and he recanted his identification of the Twins as the shooters. He later told investigators that Mills-Francis had paid him $260 to lie. During the trial, he reverted back to his original testimony, but the damage had been done. He had given three different versions, and jurors don't like that.

"Ridiculous," Mills-Francis said in an interview in the *Miami Herald*. "I did not pay him a dime." Later, in the same interview, though, she acknowledged that she had paid the witness "cab fare" on several occasions.

The acquittal of the Twins forced our hand. We couldn't let them back out on the streets, so we charged them with the attempted murders of Rah-Rah and assorted narcotics violations.

Prosecutor Chris Clark was concerned about the cozy relationship Karen Mills-Francis had with the Boobie Boys. In a motion to the court, he sought to have her barred from defending any of the Bobbie Boys during the upcoming CCE. He cited what he called an obvious conflict of interest. He even went as far as to say that Mills-Francis herself might become a target of the investigation, or at the very least, a material witness, because of her vast knowledge of the organization. In his brief Chris wrote:

Via this motion, the government has notified attorney Mills-Francis of her status as a subject before an ongoing grand jury investigation related to the activities on behalf of Lenard Brown and others.

He also issued a grand jury subpoena for Mills-Francis ordering her to appear at the next session. One of the requirements of the subpoena was that she bring all her fee records pertaining to the Boobie Boys.

That night, I delivered the subpoena to her home in the northeast section of Miami-Dade. When I formally served her with the summons, she angrily snatched it from my hand and slammed her front door in my face.

When the time came for her to testify before the grand jury, she refused. She invoked her Fifth Amendment right against self-incrimination. After some bartering, she revealed that her reluctance to testify stemmed from a $30,000 payment she had received from the Twins' mother. She had not claimed the money on her income tax or informed the IRS of its source. It was an act of omission not evasion, she said. When asked if she knew the source of the $30,000, she said the Twins' father told her he had won the money gambling, and she believed him.

Several weeks later, I was standing in the homicide break room pouring a cup of coffee when Joe Malott walked in behind me. "You're not going to believe this, Sarge," he said. "SRT has Karen Mills-

Francis' house surrounded. Apparently, her husband has threatened to kill her, and shots have been fired."

By the time I got there, it was all over. Her husband, Arthur Francis, had taken her hostage and had shot at the SWAT team when they surrounded the house. Negotiators tried to reason with Francis, but he ended up killing himself with a single gunshot to the head. Officers told me Mills-Francis was injured but not severely. I scanned the scene and spotted Karen sitting in the back of a Fire Rescue vehicle being attended to. As I watched her sobbing, I actually felt sorry for her.

Figure 32. Karen Mills-Francis (IMDb)

CHAPTER 15
Bubba and Little Bo

The John Doe Boys took their name from the toe tags attached to the unidentified bodies at the morgue. Corey Smith (AKA Bubba) was their leader, and they controlled a large swath of Liberty City including the lucrative Pork and Bean projects and the notorious "15th Avenue." One of Bubba's main lieutenants was a female named Peggy King. Other lieutenants and enforcers had colorful nicknames such as: Jew Dog, Garhead, Crazy E, Little Bo, Manny Boo, and Scooby.

At the same time the North End Task Force was trying to dismantle the Boobie Boys and Vonda's Gang, the city of Miami had formed their own task force to stop the violence perpetrated by the John Doe Boys. Lieutenant John Campbell from the City of Miami homicide section was put in charge. The city dedicated a sergeant and 13 detectives to the John Doe Task Force, who teamed up with the FBI and the U.S. Attorney's Office.

The John Does were believed to be responsible for at least two dozen murders and many more woundings. Because the violence was not always confined to the City of Miami's jurisdiction, but often spilled over into Miami-Dade County, Sergeant Mike Fisten from the Northside District was assigned to assist their task force.

Mike worked on my squad for many years while we were in the Robbery Bureau. He spent several years in homicide before being promoted to sergeant and was an excellent detective. After serving 25 years with MDPD, he retired and became a private investigator.

In 2009, he was hired by an attorney representing the families of numerous underage victims who had been sexually molested by a vile pedophile. Mike spent the next decade amassing an ironclad case against Jeffrey Epstein who was arrested in 2019. Had it not been for Mike's diligence and perseverance, that despicable monster would never have been brought to justice. It was Mike who made the prosecution of

Jeffrey Epstein possible.

Just like Boobie and Vonda, the John Doe Boys were locked in a violent dispute with the Cloud Nine Gang, over drug turf. Cory "Bubba" Smith had a reputation on the streets as being untouchable because he had skated on most of his arrests, including a first-degree murder charge.

Bubba was arrested in November of 1996 for the murder of 19-year-old Dominique Johnson, a rival drug dealer. Johnson was sitting on a bus bench with headphones on listening to music when Bubba snuck up behind him and opened fire with an automatic pistol. Johnson was hit in the head, neck, shoulders, and upper back. He died on the scene.

The key witness against Bubba was Cynthia Brown, who watched the entire incident from her front porch. Knowing Bubba's reputation and fearing for her life and the safety of her three young children, Brown avoided the police for three months. She finally came forward and identified Corey "Bubba" Smith as the killer.

Incredibly, Bubba was released on a mere $50,000 bond. This was unheard of in an execution style first-degree murder charge. David Waxman, the prosecutor on the case, was quoted as saying, "I can't remember the last guy on trial for first-degree murder where the state was seeking the death penalty being let out on bond."

Two days before the trial of Corey "Bubba" Smith was set to begin, Cynthia Brown, mother of three, was found murdered in a Little Havana hotel room. Four days later, charges were dropped against Bubba. Without her, the state no longer had a case.

Homicide detectives are known for minimizing the risks of testifying in a murder trial and reassuring reluctant witnesses that they will not be harmed. We tell frightened witnesses, "You've been watching too much TV. Nothing ever happens to witnesses. You will be completely safe."

But it's a big lie. Witnesses *are* murdered. Five were murdered in the Boobie Boys investigation alone. Not only are they killed, but they are also beaten, kidnapped, shot, stabbed, bribed and at the very least, harassed. Their family members can be killed, threatened, kidnapped, and assaulted. Several witnesses in Miami-Dade County have been blown up in their cars with explosives. It doesn't just happen in the movies or on TV.

Prosecutor David Waxman told the *Miami Herald*:

On the eve of a very serious murder trial our only eyewitness has been killed. A very courageous woman has been killed because she wanted to do the right thing. Cynthia was afraid for her life. She knew the kind of danger she was putting herself in. But she said, 'It wasn't right what he did to that boy. I'll testify.'

In the latter part of 1998, Miami-Dade County exploded with violence over a rift between two childhood friends. Cory Smith (AKA Bubba) and Anthony Fail (AKA Little Bo) grew up together in a section of Liberty City known as Model City. As teenagers, they formed a gang called the

Lynch Mob that eventually morphed into the John Doe Boys. Unhappy with his position in the John Doe Boys, Little Bo decided to strike out on his own and form his own drug distribution posse, in direct competition with Bubba. He also began robbing the John Doe drug holes. Little Bo acquired his nickname as a child. He was always short and bowlegged. He wore his hair in a de-la-sol cut, named after rapper De La Soul.

The dispute resulted in over a dozen shootings in a two-week period. The evening news was replete with reports of murders, drive-by shootings, and wounded victims.

Houses occupied by John Doe members were riddled with bullets. Antonio Godfrey (AKA Garhead), the fourth in command of the John Doe Boys, was shot and paralyzed while walking down 62nd Street. Thirty-five rounds from an AK-47 were fired into one residence, and ten people were hit including a nine-year-old girl. Most of the shootings were attributed to Little Bo.

In retaliation, Little Bo's girlfriend,

Angel Wilson, was killed. Fifteen bullets from a .223 rifle ripped through her body while she was seated in her Honda Accord. Fifty spent shell casings were found near her car. She left behind a five-year-old son.

In a six-week period, eleven people were murdered, five in one week. Most of the slayings were on or near Northwest 15th Avenue.

The community was incensed. The City of Miami Police Department declared war on those responsible and dedicated 25 officers exclusively to an initiative christened *"Operation Draw The Line"* to stop the violence. Little Bo was their main target and they launched one of the most intensive manhunts the city of Miami had ever seen.

As part of the investigation, a search warrant was served on the residence of Corey "Bubba" Smith, the leader of the John Does. Multiple firearms and two live hand grenades were seized. Search warrants at the home of Smith's sister produced a Ruger Mini-14 rifle, a Mac-10 machine pistol, a MAC-90 rifle, $186,000 in cash, a diamond studded Rolex watch, and a 75 round capacity drum magazine for an AK-47. As a convicted felon, Smith faced life in federal prison for possession of guns and explosive devices if he was found guilty.

The search for Little Bo consumed South Florida. A huge reward was offered for his apprehension. Radio and TV stations would interrupt their programming with information about the latest sighting of Little Bo. Eight days into the search with hundreds of tips checked out, Little Bo was still a fugitive.

Unbelievably, it was Rah-Rah who was responsible for the capture of Little Bo. He had been transferred from Macon, Georgia to the Federal Detention Center in Miami, and he somehow learned in a telephone call with an unidentified female where Little Bo was hiding. He called his prosecutor AUSA Mike Solis in Macon collect, hoping to curry favor with him. He told Mike that Little Bo was hiding out at a Days Inn in Palm Beach County. Mike called the task force, and they surrounded the Days Inn where they nabbed Little Bo.

Little Bo was returned to Miami where he gave a twelve-hour confession to investigators implicating many of the John Doe Boys. The next day, two hundred police officers fanned out across Miami-Dade County and arrested 25 people associated with the John Doe Boys and the Cloud Nine Gang. It appeared to the public that the arrests were made as a direct result of Little Bo's confession, but it was just a coincidence. The indictments were months in the making and had been decided long before he made his admissions.

The multi-count CCE indictment contained five murders, including the murder of Cynthia Brown. Court documents showed that the task force had obtained pen registers and wire taps and had listened to over 2,500 phone calls made by Cory Smith. Most of them were narcotics transactions.

In a statement to the press, Tom Scott, the U.S. Attorney of the Southern District of Florida, said:

These two indictments represent a major blow to two of the most significant narcotics gangs operating in Liberty City, and in the case of the John Doe organization, perhaps, by far the most violent. Some of you may say, won't another gang just step up and take the place of the John Does and the Cloud Nines of the world? If they are willing to face life in prison, we're willing to take them on.

After five years of legal wrangling, Cory Smith was found guilty of the five murders he had been charged with, including that of Cynthia Brown, Angel Wilson, and a deaf mute named Jackie Pope. My good friend, George Cholakis, was the prosecutor. The trial lasted 33 days and the state called 84 witnesses. Little Bo, who was serving two life sentences, testified against Bubba.

Because of numerous threats, two armed police officers searched all individuals, including jurors, who entered the hallway outside the courtroom. Multiple armed police officers were stationed inside and outside the courtroom. Smith was required to wear a stun belt. Spectators had to present photo identification before being admitted to the courtroom.

Although he was already serving a life term in federal prison for drug trafficking, the judge imposed two death sentences on Bubba for the murders of Cynthia Brown and Angel Wilson. He was sent to death row to await his execution.

Then in 2017, his death sentences were vacated by the Hurst decision. In Hurst v. State, the Florida Supreme Court ruled that all death sentences required a unanimous jury recommendation. The jury recommendation for Cynthia Brown was 10-2, and for Angel Wilson, the recommendation was 9-3.

Bubba was re-sentenced to multiple life terms and will never see daylight outside of prison walls again.[45]

---

[45] From Robert Lee Sawyer's plea agreement.

CHAPTER 16
Zeus and Flave

Several days after the Mother's Day article appeared in the *Miami Herald*, I received a phone call from DEA agent Charlie Gravatte in Pensacola. He told me that the article had been brought to his attention by one of his informants. He said that he had been building a trafficking in narcotics case against one of the individuals mentioned in the clipping... Jesus "Zeus" Wilson. According to Charlie, he had amassed enough evidence against Zeus to put him in federal prison for the rest of his life, and a warrant for his arrest had been issued.

This was welcome news since our informants had been telling us over and over that Zeus was "weak" and would definitely rollover on the Boobie Boys if he faced jail time. Zeus had a wife and a four-year-old son that he doted on. Life in prison was certainly not in his plans.

(Sixteen years later, Jesus Wilson, Jr. would be the starting wide receiver and record holding punt returner for the Florida State Seminoles).

Charlie faxed me a copy of the warrant, and the task force began searching for Zeus. Within hours, Chuck Clark spotted him in Carol City driving a blue Saab. He followed the Saab into a residential area near Northwestern High School where he took Zeus into custody. At the homicide office, he was read his rights and didn't hesitate to give up the Boobie Boys.

Zeus explained that he was more of an associate member of the Boobie Boys and not part of their inner circle. He always felt that Boobie never completely trusted him after Gerry Dukes was murdered at his barber shop. Nevertheless, he still knew a lot. He said that numerous homicides were discussed openly in front of him. He recalled being at the One-of-a-Kind Bar the day Wallace Fortner was murdered in Overtown. E-4, Marvin Rogers, and Vinnie (Vincent Delaveux) came into the bar, and E-4 shouted triumphantly, "We got him!"

The trio then animatedly explained how they killed Fortner. They said they had waited outside his house in a stolen car and when he came out, they cut him down with "choppers." Vinnie and E-4 told Zeus that the city of Miami police stopped them leaving the scene of the shooting but let them go, not even checking to see if their vehicle was stolen. The AK-47s they used to kill Fortner were in the trunk, but the police officers never looked.

He also knew about the murders of Tyrone Tarver and Roger Davis at the Amoco gas station on 62nd Street. He said the shooters were E-4 and Death (Richard Stitt) and that the AK-47s used were supplied by his friend Roshawn Davis. (This was later confirmed in an interview I conducted with Roshawn Davis on February 1, 2001).

He went on to say that Nard and Shotout were responsible for the shooting at Vonda's duplex on New Years Day, in which Vonda's boyfriend Pookalotta was paralyzed. He knew about this incident firsthand because he was one of the getaway drivers. He had also been told about all the attempts on Rah-Rah's life and that Boobie and Marvin Rogers killed Bennie Brownlee.

Finally, he said the Twins bragged to him on numerous occasions that they were guilty of the murder of John Davis for which they had been acquitted. To save himself, he said he was willing to testify about all he knew. He would make a great witness. That is, if we could just keep him alive.

Zeus and Charlton Dacres (AKA Flave) met each other in high school. After graduation Flave got his girlfriend pregnant so her father, who was a longshoreman, secured a job for him working on the docks at the Port of Miami. Flave eventually joined the longshoremen's union.

The Port of Miami is located at the mouth of the Miami River in Biscayne Bay. It is the largest passenger port in the world and one of the largest cargo ports in the United States. It accounts for 340,000 jobs and has an overall economic impact of $45 billion to the state of Florida. Designated the "Cargo Gateway of the Americas," it is the largest container port in the state of Florida and ninth largest in the United States. Over 10 million tons of cargo pass through the Port of Miami every year.

Shortly after he started working at the Port, Flave met a fellow longshoreman known as Heavy. Under Heavy's tutelage, Flave learned how to smuggle drugs off the Port. The drugs would usually arrive in the United States hidden in cargo containers but were also smuggled into the country by cruise ship employees. Within 18 months, Flave was moving 50 to 80 kilos at a time to Heavy's house in North Miami. The shipments were sporadic but generally came in every six months or so and were typically on ships arriving from Panama. The value of each shipment in today's money would be over $2 million.

Although Flave was paid for his efforts, it was Heavy who received the bulk of the profits. Flave soon learned that Heavy's connection was a Panamanian named

Carlos Blanco. He found out that Blanco had a house in Miami Lakes, so he contacted Blanco and offered to deal with him directly. Blanco agreed to the arrangement because he felt Heavy was being "too cautious" and only wanted to import small quantities "to keep a low profile." Blanco wanted to move more weight than Heavy was willing to risk.

Plus, Flave had just been arrested for stealing two jet skis from the Port. His truck had been impounded and he owed $9,000 in legal fees. He was flat broke and tried to borrow money from several people, all of whom turned him down. A friend of his from high school, Ronald Raye (AKA Rollo), introduced him to Boobie. He explained his new drug connection with Blanco to Boobie and Boobie agreed to loan him the $9,000 with the understanding that he would pay him back with cocaine.

Within a week, Carlos Blanco notified Flave that 500 kilos would be arriving at the Port on the *Seaboard Universe*, a cargo ship from Panama. (500 kilos would have a street value in today's money of $15 million).

Flave snuck the 500 kilos off of the Port and delivered them to Blanco. Blanco gave him ten kilos out of the 500 as payment. That afternoon, he sold all ten kilos to Boobie for $150,000. Boobie subtracted the $9,000 Flave owed from the amount and gave him $141,000 in cash. Within a couple of hours, Boobie called Flave and said he wanted to buy another 10 kilos. Blanco agreed to front the 10 kilos to Flave. Boobie showed up with the money and paid for the kilos. In a few short hours, Flave had collected $291,000 in cash that he stuffed into several duffel bags and locked in the trunk of his car.

That evening, Boobie called Flave and said that he wanted to purchase twenty more kilos. Blanco again agreed to front the dope. Rollo and Wayne Baptiste showed up at Flave's house with a duffel bag containing what was supposed to be $300,000. Flave gave them the 20 Kilos and began counting the money on his back patio.

Just as he realized that he was $40,000

short, three armed men clad in ski masks jumped over his back fence and began shooting at him. He grabbed the bag containing the money and fled through his house and out the front door. Shots were still being fired at him as he used his key fob to open the trunk of his Acura Legend. He tossed the bag in and slammed the trunk lid.

He fled across the street between several houses. Minutes later he circled back and crept into his neighbor's yard where he hid behind some bushes. He watched as the masked gunmen shot out the windows of his Acura and reached in and popped the trunk. He clearly recognized one of the masked robbers as Wayne Baptiste, who had delivered the money earlier. The other two he believed to be Boobie and E-4.

As they started removing the duffel bags from the trunk, Flave pulled a .380 pistol from his waistband and began firing. The three robbers shot back but fled. When Flave checked his trunk, he found one duffel bag containing $96,000 had been left behind by the thieves.

Flave had been naïve. He knew Boobie's reputation for robbing dope dealers, but he thought it would never happen to him. He thought Boobie would welcome the steady supply of cocaine he could provide and deal with him honestly. But with Boobie, greed always took over.

To cover his ass, Flave made a police report. Luckily for him, the shooting incident occurred in a quiet residential neighborhood and made the evening news. This convinced Carlos Blanco that the robbery was real. Even though Blanco was furious with him, he agreed to let him work off the money he had lost.

Two days later, Flave knocked on Rollo's door demanding the $40,000 that he had been shorted. Boobie was with Rollo and told Flave, "If I wanted to rob you, I would have killed you. If I keep hearing that you say I robbed you, I will come back and kill you." Flave decided to let it go.

Flave gave Carlos Blanco the $96,000 he had managed to rescue from the trunk and signed the title of his Acura Legend over to him, but Blanco shunned him and gave him no more work. Instead, Blanco began collaborating with Zeus. It was Flave who introduced the two to each other. Blanco preferred working with Zeus because Zeus spoke fluent Spanish, and he could send him to Panama to negotiate the deals.

Desperate for money, Flave contacted Carlos Blanco's uncle in Panama whom he called "Unk." After several phone conversations, Unk invited Flave to Panama to set up a smuggling operation. Fearing he was being set up by Carlos Blanco and would be killed in Panama, Flave sent his cousin, Alphonso Carter, in his place. Carter used Flave's passport since he didn't have one, replacing Flave's picture with his. Everything went well with Unk, and the smuggling activities at the Port continued.

Relying on information furnished by Zeus, Chris Clark filed charges against Flave and his cousin for using fraudulent passports to facilitate narcotics transactions. By the time of their arrests in December of 1998, they had smuggled more than 900 kilos of cocaine through the

Port of Miami. They were both found guilty, and each received 20 years in federal prison.

Following his sentencing, Flave attempted to commit suicide in the courthouse holding facility. He tore cloth strips from his prison jumpsuit to create a ligature and tried to hang himself. U.S. Marshalls found him hanging and cut him down.

Zeus and Carlos Blanco continued their association until Blanco was arrested. Through connections he had at Port Everglades in Ft. Lauderdale they were able to smuggle cocaine into both locations. Zeus estimated that they were able to move over 1,000 kilos of cocaine through both ports. At least 200 of those were sold to Boobie. Most of the profit went to Blanco, of course, who had to pay his sources in Panama, but Zeus usually received $800 to $1,000 per kilo. Kilos at the time were selling anywhere from $14,000 to $18,000 depending upon demand and availability.

DEA agents in Miami arrested Carlos

Blanco at his home and seized seven kilos. Blanco pleaded guilty to drug trafficking and was sentenced to 15 years in federal prison.

Zeus was taken to Pensacola where he pleaded guilty to trafficking in cocaine and was sentenced to life in prison. The judge allowed him to enter into a Rule 35 with the understanding that if he testified truthfully in the Boobie Boys case, his life sentence would be reduced significantly, but no less than 15 years.[46]

---

[46] From court testimony and interviews with Charlton Dacres conducted by Det. Joe Malott, Det. Mike Hernandez, and DEA agent Lenny Athas.

CHAPTER 17
Vinnie

Throughout the spring of 1999, we continued presenting evidence and witnesses to the grand jury. We de-briefed hundreds of individuals, mostly federal inmates, to determine their fitness to testify. We also tried to corroborate as much of what they told us as we could.

For example, Detectives Joe Malott and Dave Simmons spoke with federal inmate Dante Harris who was originally from Raleigh, North Carolina. He said that before he was arrested, his roommate in a house on Watkins Street was a man named Clarence Hill. The lease on the residence was paid for by Bernard Shaw, one of Boobie's lieutenants and one of his closest boyhood friends. Hill told Harris that he and Bernard Shaw were half-brothers.

Harris agreed to transport kilos of cocaine for Shaw to North Carolina for distribution in and around Raleigh. He would travel to Miami where he would pick up one to three kilos of cocaine from Bernard Shaw or Ronald Raye (AKA Rollo), hide it in his Chevy Caprice, and drive back to Raleigh. While he was in Miami, he would always stay at the Holiday Inn near Calder Racetrack. Sometimes, the cocaine was in the form of crack and sometimes it was powder. He said that he made roughly 35 such trips. He would hide the drugs in the blower vent of his automobile's air conditioner.

At times, Harris would use Western Union to wire payment for the drugs back to either Shaw or Rollo. He estimated that he wired at least $100,000 in this manner. Harris also kept a ledger that recorded all his transactions with Shaw and Rollo. He believed that his mother still had the ledger.

On the last trip he made he was stopped on I-95 and arrested by the St. Lucie County Sheriff's Office who found over 1,500 grams of crack (1½ kilos) hidden in his AC vent. DEA took over his case. He was convicted and sentenced to 15 years in federal prison. At his trial, it was brought up that there was an unidentified fingerprint that had been found on the wrapper of the cocaine.

Once we heard the story, the legwork began. I subpoenaed the Western Union records. DEA agent Lenny Athas drove to Port St. Lucie, picked up the latent fingerprint card, and brought it to our ID section. Fingerprint expert George Hertel promptly compared it to a standard of Bernard Shaw. It was a perfect match.

Jeff Lewis and I served a subpoena on the Calder Holiday Inn and obtained all the records pertaining to Dante Harris. It was confirmed that he stayed there on two dozen separate occasions over a three-year period. Numerous calls from his room were made to the home numbers of Bernard Shaw and Ronald Raye. The lease on the house on Watkins Street in Raleigh was received via a subpoena and showed that Bernard Shaw did, in fact, make the rent payments.

This was the paradigm that we used for all the witnesses who said they transacted dope with the Boobie Boys. We always endeavored to find some piece of evidence that verified their stories.

We compiled a list of relevant questions, such as: Were you ever arrested with the dope? Were you ever stopped by the police? Did you ever get a ticket or warning? Where did you stay? What phones did you use? Do you have any receipts from the trips? Did you wire any money? Did anything unusual happen? Anything that could be checked out to support their testimony.

In the case of Dante Harris, we hit the jackpot when his mother handed over the ledger he had kept. It was very detailed and listed years of illegal transactions with the Boobie Boys.

There were so many witnesses that we tendered to the grand jury that two additional U.S. Attorneys had to be assigned to help with the workload. Stacey Levine and Bruce Brown began by de-briefing witnesses, preparing their testimony, and authoring indictments and search warrants. As it turned out, they eventually became permanent members of our task force, and along with Chris Clark did a phenomenal job. The three of them were a true "dream team," and without them, it is doubtful that the case would have had the success that it did.

The grand jury would meet every Thursday, from 9 a.m. to 5 p.m. Following each session, the rush hour traffic back to the headquarters building was always an impenetrable parking lot, so we would meet at Tobacco Road for beers and steaks, until it cleared.

Tobacco Road is Miami's oldest saloon. It has survived several Miami land booms, Al Capone, prohibition, the Great Depression, two world wars, countless deadly hurricanes, the Mariel Boatlift, race-riots, and the cocaine cowboys. When you walked in the front door, you could see the very first liquor license issued by the City of Miami in 1912, number 001, encased in a small frame hanging on the wall. It was located near the Miami River, and the back patio offered a magnificent view of the Miami skyline at night. The nightly special on Thursdays was the T-bone steak; a huge hunk of meat accompanied by French fries and a salad, all for $6.99.

Boobie Boy, James Vincent Deleveaux (AKA Vinnie), was charged with two separate firearms cases. He decided to fight the first one. At the conclusion of the three-day trial in the courtroom of Judge James Lawrence King the twelve-member jury returned a verdict of guilty in a matter of ten minutes. Karen Mills-Francis represented Vinnie.

Following the guilty verdict, she approached ATF special agent, Carlos Canino, in the hallway in front of Judge King's courtroom and expressed a willingness on the part of her client to cooperate. The sentencing guidelines called for five years, but Judge King was expected to depart from the guidelines and impose a 15-year sentence due to Vinnie's association with the Boobie Boys. Plus, he had been convicted in 1990 for attempted first degree murder and had served 7 years in state prison.

Vinnie still had another federal firearms indictment pending. This was the case where he was caught with E-4 and Boobie in the city of Miami when all three were enroute to kill Vonda and Rah-Rah. City of Miami police officers tried to stop their stolen vehicle, and they fled. During the pursuit, they threw an H&K rifle, an Uzi sub machine gun, and a Ruger .223 rifle out of the windows, along with body armor, ski masks, and gloves. A Miami police K-9 located them hiding in a tool shed not far from where they bailed out of the stolen car.

To solidify the case, search warrants were served on both E-4 and Vinnie to obtain their DNA. Dave Simmons and Associate Medical Examiner Valerie Rao presented the warrants to them at the Federal Detention Center in downtown Miami. With the help of SIS personnel, E-4 and Vinnie were taken to the medical facility in the detention center where a tube of venous blood was drawn from each of them by Dr. Rao. Two saliva swabs were also taken.

The MDPD crime lab extracted Vinnie and E-4's DNA from the blood and saliva and linked it to DNA found on the ski masks and gloves thrown from the vehicle. If Vinnie was convicted on this case, and the evidence against him looked awfully strong, he could receive 40 more years.

While locked up and awaiting his second trial, he was full of confidence and bravado. He told fellow inmate Dennis Bell, "Boobie is going to take care of all this. As soon as the witness list comes out, Boobie is going to have their families killed. He still has plenty of killers out there that can do the job. We know about Zeus. Boobie put a $200,000 hit out on him."

Vinnie also told Bell about an incident where he, Boobie, Marvin Rogers, the Twins, and E-4, tried to kill Rah-Rah in Overtown. Rah-Rah returned fire and struck Marvin directly in the chest twice but he was wearing a bullet proof vest and that saved his life.

Chris Clark subpoenaed Vinnie to testify before the grand jury about his involvement with the Boobie Boys, but when the Marshals brought him to the grand jury room, he refused to say anything. He was taken immediately to the courtroom of Judge Patricia Seitz who had issued the subpoena. Prosecutor Bruce Brown informed Judge Seitz of Vinnie's refusal to testify and she held him in contempt of court. What that meant for Vinnie was that as long as he was in contempt, he would begin serving "dead time." That is, the clock stopped. He was in limbo. Time stood still for him, and no time would come off his firearms sentence.

In a subsequent interview with ATF agent Canino, he told him that his refusal to testify was based on principle. He said he had a reputation to uphold; that he was known as a soldier and a "respected robber", and snitches were simply cowards. When agent Canino told him his silence could result in more prison time he shouted, "I don't give a shit! Bring it on! Give me more time!"

He did eventually cooperate with the task force and furnish some basic background information, but he still refused to testify against anyone. In the end, Vinnie pleaded guilty and was given 15 years in federal prison, his reputation intact.[474849]

---

[47] Judge King is still on the bench. He is the senior United States district judge of the United States District Court for the Southern District of Florida, and one of the longest serving federal judges in the United States.

[48] From court testimony and an interview with Dennis Bell conducted by the author.

[49] From Courtroom testimony and interviews conducted with Dante Harris and Jimmy Mills by Detectives Jeff Lewis, Joe Malott, Mike Hernandez, Sgt. Dave Simmons, and DEA special agent Lenny Athas.

PART FOUR

CHAPTER 18
CCE

Preparing for the Continuing Criminal Enterprise (CCE) indictments was tedious and time-consuming. Chris Clark made a tactical decision to concentrate solely on the Boobie Boys for the CCE and dismantle Vonda's Gang with firearms and narcotics violations. If the Boobie Boys case was successful, we planned to initiate a similar CCE for Vonda's Gang.

In a little over one year, the task force had interviewed hundreds of witnesses and culled out the weak or undesirable ones. Even so, we still presented 120 witnesses to the grand jury. Each witness that made the cut had to be re-interviewed two or three times. And with information obtained from each witness, the case expanded and burgeoned even more.

Each potential witness had to be vetted for *Giglio* and *Brady* violations, two

Supreme Court decisions that pertained to witness testimony. In *Giglio v. United States*, the court held that the jury must be informed of any promises made to the witness in exchange for his or her testimony. This was fairly straight forward. The Brady decision, though, was more complicated.

Brady v. Maryland (1963) was a landmark decision in which the court ruled that the prosecutor must turn over to the defense any evidence that might tend to exonerate a defendant. This is known as exculpatory evidence, i.e., evidence that is favorable to the defendant and could possibly sway a jury to find him not guilty.

The facts of the Brady case are interesting. In 1958, John Brady and Charles Boblit killed William Brooks. Brady admitted being involved but claimed that it was Boblit who did the actual killing.

Brady said they stole Brooks's car to use in a bank robbery. They placed a log across the road leading to Brooks' house, and when Brooks's got out of his car to move the log, they hit him over the head with a shotgun. They drove him to a secluded area where either Brady or Boblit strangled Brooks to death with a shirt.

After being arrested, they both gave several different statements in which the facts changed repeatedly; however, Brady consistently denied killing Brooks and always maintained that it was Boblit who strangled him.

Prior to Brady's murder trial, Brady's lawyer asked the prosecutor for any admissions either of the men had made. The prosecutor turned over all Boblit's statements except one in which he confessed to killing the victim. Both Brady and Boblit were convicted in separate trials and sentenced to death.

The Maryland Court of Appeals held that "suppression by the prosecutor of evidence favorable to the accused violates due process." The United States Supreme Court concurred and said that "the Constitution requires the disclosure of exculpatory evidence."

Over the years, thousands of felons have been released from prison due to Brady violations that were uncovered after they were convicted. The interpretation of what is considered "exculpatory" though is ambiguous. Any prior arrests must be disclosed. If the witness ever used an alias or gave the wrong date of birth to the police, this could be considered lying and something the jury should know about. If the witness ever denied the charges against him in court and was later convicted, that could be construed as lying under oath.

Our witnesses were certainly not saints. And for them lying to the police was a way of life. Chris Clark and I spent countless hours combing the arrest affidavits and police reports trying to find information that needed to be disclosed. The discovery material we had to furnish to the defense lawyers became massive.

We had to make copies of everything and then use a Bates stamp to mark the pages. A Bates stamp sequentially numbers all the documents. Starting at 00000, the stamp advances by one digit each time it is pressed down on the page and leaves an inked imprint of that number. By the time of the trial, we had turned over tens of thousands of pages of material.

The volume of paperwork we were generating was becoming problematic. Sergeant Dave Simmons had created files on all of our targets and witnesses, and by mid-May, he was up to 600 folders. We didn't have enough space to accommodate all our files and evidence. Chris Clark convinced the Marshals to allow us to occupy a windowless room in the old courthouse known as the Igloo. It was called the Igloo because it was a room that was always cold. Even on the hottest Miami days, the air conditioner pumped Arctic frigid air out of the vents until it felt like you were in, well, an igloo. We called it our "war room."

Figure 33. Working in the Igloo. Left to right, Jeff Lewis, Dave Simmons, the author, Bruce Brown, Joe Malott, Mike Hernandez, Stacey Levine, and Chris Clark. Missing are Chuck Clark, Lenny Athas, and Carlos Canino.

On May 6, 1999, the Boobie Boys grand jury returned an 18 count CCE indictment naming 15 defendants: Kenneth Williams (AKA Boobie), Efrain Casado (AKA E-4), Leonard Brown (AKA Bo), Lenard Brown (AKA Nard), Susan Hall Gibson (AKA Miss Sue), Bernard Shaw, Marvin Baker, Malcolm Shaw (AKA Rat), Ronald Raye (AKA Rollo), Wayne Baptiste (AKA Fat Wayne), Michael Harper (AKA Chico), Arthur Pless (AKA Plex), Ben Johnson (AKA Bush), Johnathon Hawthorne (AKA Moose) and Charlton Dacres (AKA Flave).

Included in the formal accusation were 15 murders. The names of the victims are listed below:

- Bennie Brownlee
- Walter Betterson
- Derick Young
- Everette Cooper
- Otis Green
- Alice Gardener
- Michael Frazier (5 years of age)
- Moses Brown
- Tarvis Miller
- Johnny Beliard
- Roger Davis
- Tyrone Tarver
- Alvin Kelly
- Roosevelt Davis
- John Davis, Jr.

The indictment was signed by the foreperson of the grand jury and by the Assistant United States Attorneys, Chris Clark, Bruce Brown, and Stacey Levine. It was the culmination of a year and a half of incredibly hard work. Those of us on the task force were elated, but we also knew that there was a lot more work to do. We had to find all these mutts and arrest them, then prepare for the eventual trial.

We spent the weekend planning for the arrests. DEA agents, ATF agents, and Miami-Dade plain clothes and uniform personnel were assigned to teams responsible for hitting the houses of each of the 11 individuals who were still at large. E-4, Flave, Bo, and Nard were already in custody.

We struck at dawn, conducting coordinated raids. In his book *Street Kings of Miami*, Seth Ferranti describes the takedowns this way:

The feds were all over them. They came at them hard. First they swept through Little River, then they shook down Liberty City. At the same time, they were in Carol City. The raids were simultaneous involving all branches of the government law enforcement agencies. All the alphabet boys came out. By the time they got finished locking people up, questioning them and inflicting their Gestapo tactics, the

Boobie Boys were done. They went from running the streets to being confined in jail cells.

The Boobie Boys were down but not out. They were getting ready to rumble with the feds in federal court. The United States of America versus the Boobie Boys. It would be their toughest battle yet. Because with the feds there was no quarter given, no quarter taken. The rough streets of MIA had left the Boobie Boys battle tested but now they would have their hands full with the feds. They were gorillas in the street, but the feds were top dogs in the world. The gang and the government weren't so different.

Seth Ferranti is an ex-con who spent 21 years of a 25-year sentence in federal prison for possession of LSD. While locked up, he earned three college degrees including his Masters. In prison, he wrote 22 books about street gangsters, drug lords, and prison gangs. His writing is obviously anti-government and highly sympathetic to the convicts who make up the overwhelming majority of his readers. He wrote, produced, and appeared in the Netflix documentary *White Boy Rick*.

I was on the team that was assigned to arrest Ronald Raye. We woke him out of a sound sleep and when he realized what he was being charged with, he started shaking like a wet dog. At one point, I thought he might pass out. I knew there was no way he would hold up and I was right, Rollo was the first one to flip.

We took him back to the DEA office in the Koger Center and learned that the other teams had captured Wayne Baptiste, the Twins' mother, Susan Hall Gibson, the cop Marvin Baker, Malcolm Shaw, Arthur Pless. and Ben Johnson, who was in a wheelchair.

Later that day, Bernard Shaw surrendered himself to me at his lawyer's office in Ft. Lauderdale, and Johnathon Hawthorne was apprehended in Overtown. I tried to talk to Moose (Hawthorne) because he had been somewhat cooperative when I interviewed him months earlier, but he was not very friendly this time. He told me, "Maaan, get outta my face with that Homer Simpson style voice you got."

Only Boobie and Michael (Chico) Harper were still on the loose.

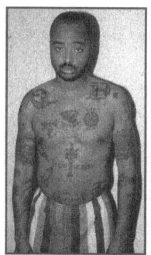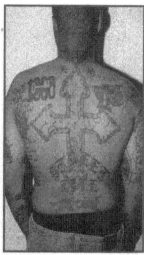

Figure 34. Arthur Pless, AKA Plex, shows off his tattoos at the DEA office after the Boobie Boys roundup. (Author)

We still couldn't find Boobie. Dozens of tips came in, but we always seemed to be a step behind him. We stopped cars, kicked in doors, and surveilled his known haunts, but he remained a fugitive. We needed help, and the United States Marshals Service agreed to detach Deputy Marshal

Mike Moran to the task force to track him down. Mike was a wizard at tracing cell phones and pre-paid phone cards. He immediately determined that Boobie was using "burner" phones, which would make finding him harder, but not impossible.

I had worked with Mike before on homicide cases and had complete confidence in him. He was a bulldog who never gave up. I knew with Mike after him, it would just be a matter of time before Boobie would be in custody.

The U.S. Marshals Service has a storied history. It is the oldest federal law enforcement agency in existence, created in 1789 during the presidency of George Washington. Their main responsibility is the protection of judges and judicial personnel as well as the apprehension of fugitives from justice. They are also tasked with operating the Federal Witness Protection Program, the execution of federal warrants, and the transportation of federal prisoners.

During the 19th century, U.S. Marshals were the only source of law enforcement throughout vast areas of the western United States. Many of those Marshals are legends today, revered for their unwavering stance against lawlessness. Wyatt Earp, Doc Holiday, Wild Bill Hickok, and Bat Masterson were all U.S. Marshals. There are currently 4,000 Deputy U.S. Marshals who capture, on average, 40,000 federal fugitives each year. They are an impressive bunch.

While Mike was working the phones, I got a call from Karen Mill-Francis. She said she had just gotten off the phone with Boobie, who told her he was willing to turn himself in within seven days, but only if all charges against the Twins were dropped. When I scoffed and told her that such an arrangement was out of the question, she said, "Well, isn't it worth two or three policeman not getting hurt or killed to let the Twins off?" I couldn't contain my anger. I told her that was an outrageous statement and that it almost sounded like a threat. (We were on a taped line, and I hoped she would go further.)

I accused her of being "bamboozled" by

her clients, and she replied, "No, no, no, that's not so. I know exactly what Boobie is capable of, and I'm sure most of what you have accused him of is true." She also said that she didn't know where Boobie was hiding but even if she did, she wouldn't tell me.

Mike Moran was closing in on Boobie. I told him about the call Boobie had made to Mills-Francis. He had been able to identify Bernard Shaw's cell phone as well as the cell phone of one of Boobie's girlfriends named Nicole. He said it appeared Boobie was hiding somewhere near Atlanta, but he was still trying to isolate the exact location.

On May 17th, 1999, (exactly a year and one week after the publication of the Mother's Day article in the *Miami Herald*), I was leaving the Federal Courthouse when my cell phone rang. The display told me it was Mike Moran.

"We got him. We got Boobie," he said excitedly. "You're the first person who knows. I wanted to call you first." Boobie was handcuffed behind the back, so he put the cell phone up to his ear, and said, "Say hi to Sergeant Monheim." Boobie refused to talk to me. All I heard him say was, "Naw man. I don't want to talk to that cracker."

Mike came back on the phone. "We got him leaving a house just outside of Atlanta. He had two kilos and two Glocks with him. The big tough-guy gangster pissed himself when we drew down on him."

CHAPTER 19
Rah-Rah

On December 17, 1999, during a routine bed check, corrections officers at FDC found one of the Twins, Nard Brown, dead in his cell. He had succumbed to an apparent heart attack. He was 21 years old.

Various informants had previously told us that Nard suffered from rheumatic heart disease and required a monthly shot at Jackson Memorial Hospital to ward off heart infections. He had rheumatic fever as a kid that damaged his heart valves. An autopsy revealed severe scarring and damage to his heart muscle as well as a faulty mitral valve.

A month prior to his death, Nard was mistakenly put in the same cell as Rah-Rah. As soon as the corrections officers walked away, Rah-Rah pounced. Nard frantically crawled under a bunk bed trying to get away but Rah-Rah grabbed him by the ankle and pulled him out. Nard screamed for the guards while Rah-Rah punched and kicked him. He was finally rescued and taken to the infirmary for treatment of his injuries. It is doubtful that the beating inflicted by Rah-Rah had anything to do with Nard's demise weeks later, but Rah-Rah bragged to other inmates that it was the "ass whipping" he gave Nard that caused his death.

Attorneys for Miss Sue (Nard's mother) and Bo (Nard's brother) filed motions requesting that they be allowed to attend the funeral. Prosecutor Chris Clark opposed the motions but was agreeable to Miss Sue attending a private viewing at the Portier Funeral Home, only if she was accompanied by U.S. Marshals. Because Bo was such a huge escape risk, Chris was averse to any type of funeral accommodations for him. In the end, Bo's request was denied, and Miss Sue was escorted by the Marshals to the funeral home for a private viewing.

Figure 35. Lenard "Nard" Brown. (Author)

Rah-Rah decided to work out the best deal he could for himself and his wife, Andrea. Andrea agreed to plead guilty to the trafficking charges in Macon, Georgia. She had a gun in the car along with several kilos when she was arrested so that bumped it up to armed trafficking. She pleaded guilty and was sentenced to 25 years in federal prison.

Prior to her sentencing, she told Detective Chuck Clark about an incident in Madison County, Florida where the sheriff's office stopped her and found two handguns in her vehicle. One was a .25 caliber pistol and the other was a 9mm Taurus. She said the 9mm was the gun that was used to kill Bear. This was the gun Rah-Rah had given to Rasheen to kill William Eland, but Rasheen killed Bear by mistake. Chuck had the Madison County Sheriff's Office test fire the weapon and FedEx three projectiles and casings to him. They were a match to the bullets removed from Bear's head at his autopsy and the casings found on the scene.

Rah-Rah entered a guilty plea to the firearms charges the task force had filed in April of 1998. He had already been sentenced to 20 years in Macon, and Federal Judge Edward Davis added another 15 to that sentence to be served consecutively. This meant he would serve a total of 35 years, and he still had the state charges for the murder of Marvin Rogers to worry about.

In a plea agreement drafted by Miami-Dade Assistant States Attorney Mike Spivak, Rah-Rah agreed to plead guilty to the murder of Rogers and receive a 20-year sentence that would run concurrent with his federal time. That is, if he testified truthfully against his co-defendants, Andre

McWhorter (Bam) and Jamal Brown (Pookalotta). He also agreed to name Vonda Jackson as the person who paid for the hit. For the first time, he acknowledged in the plea agreement that it was Vonda who paid him to kill McBride.

Rah-Rah had forewarned Vonda about his intentions. In a rambling letter, he threatened to expose her unless she sent him $5,000. Vonda turned the letter over to her probation officer who forwarded a copy to me. It is three pages long, but the pertinent section is near the end. It reads:

Black girl. I'm asking you to come up with 5 grand to go to fight for my freedom or else I am going to take the easy way out by telling everything I know about you, and all the killing you hired me to do. Which is a total of 4, not to mention how your lover killed Cabo in front of your drug hole. So don't make me go there cause we both know I've got enough to put you on Death Row, so if I'm gonna die in here, then we will both die together. Now you can take this as a joke as if the whole thing is a game, but I promise you will regret it later when you see me sitting on that stand.

After the plea agreement had been signed in front of Judge Jerald Bagley, ASA Spivak asked if I would take a formal statement from Rah-Rah that described the murder of Marvin Rogers in detail.

Two days later, I drove homicide stenographer, Joani Barry, to the U.S. Attorney's Office. I had made prior arrangements with the Marshals to have Rah-Rah brought to one of the vacant grand jury rooms.

Rah-Rah was escorted in by three U.S. Marshals. He was wearing a red jumpsuit with his feet shackled and was secured with belly chain handcuffs. He was ushered to a chair by the Marshals who eyed him warily. As Joani set up her steno machine, I opened the Marvin Rogers case file and began leafing through the reports and the crime scene pictures.

When Rah-Rah saw the photos he said, "Hey man can I see those?"

I had intended to show them to him during his statement anyway, so I let him look. When he saw the photo of Marvin Rogers laying on his side with most of his face blown off, he smiled.

"That's some of my handiwork, right there," he said gleefully.

Rah-Rah had a deep, baritone voice. He sounded a lot like Barry White, the singer. I had talked to him on the phone several times, but this was the first time in person. As he recounted the murder of Marvin Rogers, he became animated and appeared to relish re-living it.

It was a chilling narrative, and he told it with delight. He definitely reveled in the retelling of how Roger's face exploded when he fired the AK into the back of his head. When he finished, I saw the Marshals shaking their heads in disbelief and disgust.

After the Marshals took Rah-Rah back, Joani and I rode the elevator down to the lobby, and she was uncharacteristically quiet. As we were driving back to the Headquarters building, she stared straight ahead.

Finally, she said, "Oh. My. God. Isn't

that the most horrible person you have ever met? He is pure evil!"

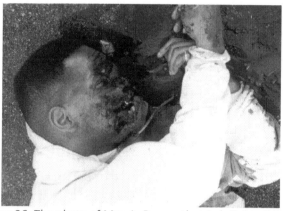

Figure 36. The photo of Marvin Rogers that Rah-Rah relished seeing. (Miami-Dade Clerk of the Court)

Rah-Rah proved to be a formidable witness. Bam and Pookalotta were both convicted of first-degree murder. Bam was sentenced to 22 years in state prison and Pookalotta to 20. Vonda was never charged by the state in the Marvin Rogers murder.

Rah-Rah was Vonda's main enforcer and hitman, of course, but she had others. One was her boyfriend, Antron Davis, known as "Tron." Since their love was eternal, Vonda had the tattoo TRON emblazoned on her chest and he had VONDA displayed on his. He also had "4Life" tattooed on the side of his neck. Not only was Tron one of Vonda's enforcers, but he was also a lieutenant in her drug organization and distribution network.

Tron was one of our first targets, and an indictment for the federal charge of possession of a firearm by a convicted felon was obtained early on. That indictment stemmed from a traffic stop that was conducted by the City of Miami Police Department. Tron was driving a Chevrolet Suburban registered to Dale Carter, a cornerback for the NFL Denver Broncos. In the Suburban, police discovered a .45 caliber automatic pistol, and he was arrested. The charges were dropped by the State Attorney's Office, of course, but re-filed at the federal level by Chris Clark and ATF agent Carlos Canino.

When the Task Force, accompanied by a bevy of ATF agents, swarmed an apartment in Overtown and arrested Tron he was in possession of an AR-15 rifle and a .12-gauge pump shotgun. As a five-time convicted felon, he was not allowed to possess any firearms, so additional charges were filed.

During an interview at the ATF field office, Tron said he and Dale Carter were roommates. He said he met Carter through Darren Mikel who was originally from Overtown and played for the San Deigo Chargers. At the time they were introduced, Carter was playing for the Kansas City Chiefs. Carter, by then, was a four-time pro bowler and had been voted Rookie Of The Year in 1992. Carter had recently purchased a house on Miami Beach, and Tron was living with him. He said they were close friends. (Tax records revealed that the house was purchased for $750,000, $1.5 million in today's money).

Four hours after Tron was arrested, Dale Carter showed up at the U.S. Attorney's Office with his lawyer. He said he was there to discuss Tron's arrest, so Assistant U.S. Attorney Karen Rocklin and I interviewed him.

According to Carter, he and Tron had been living together in a condo on Collins

Avenue for four years prior to him purchasing the house on Miami Beach. Tron also lived with him in Kansas City during the football seasons he played for the Chiefs. He said Tron often borrowed his Suburban.

While we were talking, I noticed that Carter had a "4Life" tattoo on his neck identical to Tron's. He explained that 4Life was the name of a record label he was creating, and that his brother Jake Reed, who played for the New Orleans Saints, and Fred Taylor, who played for the Jacksonville Jaguars, had the same tattoo on their necks, as did Darren Mikel. Carter said he had been traded from the Chiefs to the Broncos but had been suspended for the entire upcoming season due to an allegation of substance abuse. (Carter's son, Nigel Warrior, who was 3 years old at the time of the interview, would grow up to play cornerback for the Seattle Seahawks and the Baltimore Ravens in the NFL).

Tron was eventually convicted of all the firearms charges and sentenced to 32 years in federal prison.

After bonding with Rah-Rah at his confession, he contacted me regularly with information. One day, he called the Homicide Office and said that we needed to speak in person, not over the phone.

Because he had entered a guilty plea to the murder of Marvin Rogers, he had been transferred from FDC to the Miami-Dade County Jail. I set up the interview with the corrections staff and drove there the next day.

The only interview room available was by the fifth-floor control room near the elevators. It had a large window that faced a glass enclosed area where the cells on the floor were monitored by two jail employees.

A uniformed guard brought Rah-Rah into the room and removed his handcuffs. The only furniture was a table that was bolted to the floor and two chairs. We sat across from each other at the table and, in a low voice, Rah-Rah began telling me about a Corrections Officer (CO) who was being paid to smuggle contraband into the jail for several inmates on the third floor. He said the inmates were all members of the John Doe Boys and that the leader of the gang, Bubba Smith, was paying the CO large sums of money. Rah-Rah said the John Doe Boys were planning an escape and the CO had sold them duplicate keys and pepper spray to aid in the escape.

As I started scribbling notes onto a yellow legal pad, I was vaguely aware that five or six inmates had just gotten off the elevator and were walking by the interview room window. I glanced up and saw Rah-Rah standing over me with his chair raised over his head. He swung the chair and hit me with it on the forehead just above my left eye. The blow knocked me backwards out of my seat, and onto the floor. I covered my head with my arms as Rah-Rah continued to batter me with the chair. Luckily, I was wedged into the corner of the room and many of the intended blows struck the walls.

Three corrections officers rushed into the room, overpowered Rah-Rah, and drug him back to his cell. My head was pounding and when I touched my forehead, I felt a large lump that was getting bigger by the minute. There was no blood though. After the cobwebs cleared, I completed an arrest affidavit charging Rah-Rah with Battery on a Police Officer.

The next day, Rah-Rah called me collect, "Sarge, I'm sorry I had to do you that way, man. They was guys from my floor watching us, and I didn't want them to think I was snitching."

I was furious.

"You could have killed me, you asshole," I exaggerated.

"Naw man, I wouldn't do that. I had to make it look good. I couldn't let them think it was put on. It had to look real."

"Well, it felt real," I said. "Now, you owe me big time. You need to close some murders for me."

"You right, man. I will. I will. I promise."

Over the next two years, Rah-Rah called me faithfully and furnished information that would lead to arrests in five murders.

(I called Lieutenant Ed Cambridge who

worked Internal Affairs for the Department of Corrections and passed on what Rah-Rah had told me about the CO who was in league with the John Doe Boys. IA set up a sting and caught him red handed. He was arrested and fired, and the escape plot was foiled).

Figure 37. Robert "Rah-Rah" Sawyer. (Author)

Chapter 20
Operation Boobie Trap

Now that Boobie was finally in custody, the trial for the charge of possession of firearms by a convicted felon could proceed. Boobie and E-4 were tried together. Vinnie had already been found guilty in Judge King's courtroom.

The trial lasted two weeks and was held in the courtroom of Judge Patricia Seitz. Both Boobie and E-4 were found guilty. Judge Seitz sentenced Boobie to 18 years in federal prison and E-4 to 25 years. This took a lot of pressure off the Task Force. Should they somehow wriggle out of the CCE, we at least knew they would be off the streets for a long time.

The prosecution's case was masterfully presented by Chris Clark. I sat in for part of the proceedings and watched as he eviscerated one of Boobie's alibi witnesses. A female friend claimed he was visiting her when the police chased E-4 and Vinnie. She said Boobie just happened to be mistakenly caught up in the police perimeter. It was an absurd assertion of course, and Chris's skillful cross examination tore the alibi apart.

Boobie was represented during the court case by Miami defense attorney, Neil Nameroff. Two days after the guilty verdict, he fired Nameroff and named J. Malik Frederick of Atlanta as his lead counsel. Frederick represented Boobie at his bond hearing in Atlanta when he was arrested by the U.S. Marshals. In a strange twist, one month after being hired by Boobie, J. Malik Frederick was arrested and charged by the Feds with 10 counts of money laundering.

The CCE trial was presided over by Judge Michael Moore. Judge Moore had a reputation as a tough law-and-order jurist. From 1976 to 1989, he served as an Assistant United States Attorney in both the Northern and Southern Districts of Florida. In 1989, he was named the Director of the United States Marshal's Service and served in that capacity for four years. He was appointed to the federal bench in 1991 by President George H. W. Bush and confirmed in February of 1992.

Judge Moore oversaw a number of high-profile cases, including the money laundering trial of Miami Dolphins wide receiver, Tony Martin. Martin's co-defendant was Opa-Locka drug lord, Ricky Brownlee. A jury acquitted Martin but found Brownlee guilty, and Judge Moore sentenced him to life in federal prison.

Judge Moore also oversaw the parole hearing of Yahweh Ben Yahweh. Convicted in 1992, Yahweh Ben Yahweh (whose real name was Hulon Mitchell) was a religious cult leader who was accused of conspiring to commit 14 murders.

Right in the middle of the Boobie Boys trial, Judge Moore was asked to rule on the asylum case of Elian Gonzalez. Six-year-old Elian, his mother, and twelve other refugees left Cuba in a rickety boat attempting to seek sanctuary in the United States. A storm capsized the boat and Elian's mother, and ten others, drowned.

Young Elian was found by fisherman floating in an inner tube off the coast of Ft. Lauderdale. In a 50-page opinion, Judge Moore ruled that Gonzalez was too young to file for asylum, and asylum could only be granted by U.S. Attorney, Janet Reno.

The Boobie Boys were tried in courtroom 6-1, often referred to as the "ceremonial courtroom." It is located in the historic Post Office and Courthouse, which was constructed between 1912 and 1914. It is by far the grandest courtroom in Florida and maybe one of the most dazzling in the entire country. It is used for trials, meetings, investitures, educational seminars, chief judge elections, and other important public events. Every current and past judge in the 11th Judicial Circuit has taken his/her oath of office in Courtroom 6-1.

Courtroom 6-1 is where Al Capone was acquitted of perjury in 1930 and where Giuseppe Zangara was sentenced to death after attempting to kill Franklin D. Roosevelt in 1933 at Miami's Bayfront Park.

The bullet fired by Zangara, which was intended for President Roosevelt missed, and killed Chicago mayor Anton Cermak.

Candace Mosler and her lover/nephew accused of killing Mosler's wealthy husband were also tried in courtroom 6-1 in 1966. They were acquitted.

America's landmark tobacco trial was held in the ceremonial courtroom in the 1990s. 6-1 has been used as the courtroom backdrop in numerous movies and TV shows. Miami-Dade County Circuit Court Judge Scott Silverman explained the mystique this way, "When you get to practice law in this courtroom, everything changes. *This* is a courtroom."

The prosecution's case, put together by Chris Clark, Stacey Levine, and Bruce Brown, was nothing short of brilliant. In today's courtrooms, high-tech projection equipment allows both sides to display exhibits, controlled from a laptop, on large screens for jurors to view. In some courthouses, the judge and each juror even have their own separate monitors, but this technology was not available during the Boobie Boys trial. Chris opted to use 24"x 30" foam poster boards with photos of people, houses and businesses printed directly on them. The U.S. Attorney's Office had a printer in the basement of the building that could accommodate such large reproductions.

Jeff Lewis spent weeks driving all over Miami-Dade and Broward counties taking pictures of houses and businesses that were part of the case. Booking photos were used to identify the players. Actual crime scene photographs of the dead victims were also included.

Chris and Dave Simmons devised a clever system to retrieve the exhibits quickly when questioning each witness. There were over 300 poster board exhibits, all sequentially numbered. They were stacked in the courtroom in groups of ten. A chart was created that listed the exhibit numbers that would be needed for each witness. Before the witness took the stand, the poster board photos needed for his or her testimony were removed from the stacks. They were quickly replaced when the testimony was over.

A witness might be asked, for instance, to identify a particular house where a dope transaction took place from the oversized poster board photos, or a photo of Fish Grease as the person who sold them crack, or the One-of-a-Kind bar where they first met Boobie. This process of seeing witness after witness identify the same enlarged photos over and over, simplified the case for the jury. The defense attorneys disliked the presentation, however. E-4's attorney complained to the press saying, "All the government has are pictures of heads and houses."

The trial was a nightmare for the U.S. Marshals who were tasked with providing courtroom security. There were 11 defendants along with their lawyers seated at a long L-shaped defense table. (Of the original 15 charged in the indictment, Ronald Raye, Bernard Shaw, and Charlton Dacres had already pleaded guilty. Lenard "Nard" Brown died while awaiting trial.)

Given the violent history of the group,

the Marshals wanted all the defendants shackled with leg irons and handcuffed. The defense attorneys argued to Judge Moore that shackling and handcuffing their clients in front of the jury would be unfair and prejudicial.

Judge Moore wanted to be fair, but he was also concerned about courtroom safety, so he agreed that the defendant's legs would be manacled together but no handcuffs or restraints would be visible to the jury. A floor-length dark green tablecloth was fastened to the front of the defense table to hide the leg chains. The defendants were always moved in and out of the courtroom out of the jury's presence.

The large gallery of courtroom 6-1 was packed with spectators throughout the trial, many of whom clearly supported the Boobie Boys and looked like a group of thugs spoiling for a fight. Before entering the courtroom, each spectator was required to pass through a metal detector, but the Marshals were still concerned.

The trial began on February 7, 2000, and

lasted 37 days. The prosecution called 88 witnesses. The testimony presented evidence of the Boobie Boys' involvement in 25 murders as well as the importation and distribution of over 8,000 pounds of cocaine. Defense attorneys attacked the witnesses as "a rogues gallery of thieves, robbers, and murderers."

In his closing argument, Attorney Jason Grey who defended Moose Hawthorne, said the witness list included "50 convicts who have used 500 different names and committed 500 different crimes from obstruction to murder, and they are not believable."

Grey, who the task force nicknamed "My Cousin Vinny" because of his resemblance to Joe Pesci in the movie of the same name, told the jury that many of the witnesses had been "bribed" by the government with promises of time shaved off their sentences.

"Life sentences become 15 years, 15 years becomes five, seven becomes three. It's like dog years," he fumed. "I've never seen anything like it."

The most dramatic testimony against My

Cousin Vinnie's client, though, was not from an inmate, but from his own brother. He said that the day after the double murder at the *Amoco* station, he noticed that Moose had cut off his dreadlocks. When he asked him why, Moose replied, "I had to because of the gas station. Didn't you see the newspaper? We killed that fuck nigger Roger at the gas station. Man, we had those choppers ringing."

In his summation to the jury, Chris countered the contention that some of the witnesses had fabricated their testimony by saying, "All a big conspiracy? All the witnesses getting together and making it all up? You cannot make up anything like this. The simple answer is the truth. The government didn't pick these witnesses. The defendants did. They didn't deal with ministers. They didn't deal with judges. These are the people the defendants chose to deal with."

The jury began their deliberations on March 15, 2000. When a week had passed with no verdict, we began to worry. We all thought the case was a slam dunk. We felt the jury would see it our way and return quickly with a finding of guilty. By the eleventh day with no verdict in sight, we were downright despondent.

The defense team was suddenly all smiles. They told reporters and anyone else who would listen that the longer the jury stayed out, the more favorable it was for the defense. On day thirteen, the jury foreman informed the judge that they had reached a verdict. As we filed into the courtroom, you could tell that the lawyers and their clients were upbeat. They all sensed a win.

But when the clerk read each of the 16 counts of the indictment for each defendant, and the foreman repeatedly announced guilty to all of them, you could feel their confidence dissolving. Al Levin, attorney for Wayne Baptiste, spoke to reporters outside the courtroom after the verdicts were read.

"We're disappointed," he said. "After eight days of deliberation, we got a little excited that there was some dissension in the jury room."

When it was all over, I spoke to three of the jurors. They told me that there was never any doubt about the guilt of the defendants. Their first ballot was a unanimous guilty vote on all charges. They were just a meticulous group who wanted to weigh all the evidence carefully. They knew this was a big case, and they didn't want to be accused of rushing to judgment.

On the courthouse steps in front of the cameras, Chris, Bruce, and Stacey savored their victory before a gaggle of reporters. Chris spoke for the group and said:

"This was a special case for us because so often, you wonder whether you're really making a difference. But we have tried and convicted people who have committed more than 15 murders, delivered tons of cocaine, and corrupted a police officer. It feels good."

Following the press conference, we all adjourned to the Capitol Grill on Brickell Avenue for a celebratory dinner. We were exultant. What had started out two years earlier as the formation of a dubious task force had culminated in a resounding victory with guilty verdicts. This was the biggest case any of us had ever been involved in. None of us had ever worked harder on any investigation, and we were understandably proud of what we had accomplished.

Two months later, Judge Moore sentenced all 14 defendants as follows:

- Kenneth "Boobie" Williams --- Life in federal prison
- Efrain "E-4" Casado --- Life in federal prison
- Leonard "Bo" Brown --- Life in federal prison
- Michael "Chico" Harper --- Life in federal prison
- Johnathon "Moose" Hawthorne --- Life in federal prison
- Arthur "Plex" Pless --- Life in federal prison
- Benjamin "Bush" Johnson --- Life in federal prison
- Susan Hall Gibson --- 30 years in

federal prison

- Malcolm "Rat" Shaw --- 30 years in federal prison
- Wayne "Fat Wayne" Baptiste --- 30 years in federal prison
- Bernard Shaw --- 22 years in federal prison
- Marvin Baker ---15½ years in federal prison
- Ronald "Rollo" Raye --- 5 years in federal prison
- Charlton "Flave" Dacres --- 5 years in federal prison

Chapter 21
Rick Ross

Boobie was already a legend on the streets of Miami, but it took gangsta rapper Rick Ross to make him a national legend. As Ross put it, "Street niggas love and respect niggas that make it to the top. Everybody loves a true gangsta."

Ross was born William Leonard Roberts II and grew up in Carol City. He attended Carol City High School where he played football and hung out at the Matchbox projects. A football scholarship allowed him to attend Albany State University for four years.

In the mid-2000s, he began rapping and changed his name to Rick Ross. In 2006, he signed a recording contract with Def Jam Records and toured with Trick Daddy. His debut album, *Port of Miami*, shot up to number one on the Billboard 200. His second album in 2008, *Trilla*, also hit number one.

A track on his third album, *Valley of Death*, was specifically included to address his controversial stint as a State of Florida Corrections Officer, something he had tried to keep hidden from the public. Initially, he denied working as a CO and insisted that the photos of him in uniform were photoshopped. But when the evidence became overwhelming, he admitted it. He only held the position for 18 months, but some of his fans cried foul, calling him a fraud and a fake. He tried to justify the job and regain his "street cred" through his lyrics:

Kept a nice watch, smoking on a hundred sack
Back in the day I sold crack for some nice kicks
Skippin' school, I saw my friend stabbed with
an ice pick
Can't criticize niggas trying to get jobs
Better get smart, young brother, live yours.
Only lived once and I got two kids
And for me to feed them, I'll get two gigs
I'll shovel shit, I'll C.O.
So we can bow our heads and pray over the
meatloaf.

It's not Shakespeare, but Ross has three

gold albums and one platinum to his credit, so there are a lot of people who must think he has talent.

Many of Ross's songs pay homage to Boobie. "The dude that initially put me in the music game is Boobie," he explains. "My music touches his lifestyle. Boobie helped a lot of people in the hood and inspired a lot of positive things. The downside to it was that he was accused of over 100 homicides and running a multi-million-dollar drug enterprise."

A good deal of his lyrics refer directly to Boobie. On *Port of Miami,* he rapped, "Let me think back to '96 when Boobie had the realest nigga feeling like a bitch."

During the intro to *Trilla,* he gave, "A shoutout to Kenneth Williams. A shoutout to E-4. A shoutout to Fish Grease."

In several of his MTV videos, Ross can be seen wearing T-shirts with "Boobie Boys" written across the front. He said he wears them to honor the crew.

Ross claims that his affiliation with the Boobie Boys has inspired most of his music saying:

"The stuff I talk about is real. The dope is real. The gun talk is official. Look up Kenneth 'Boobie' Williams. Look up where he's from. That's nothing to be proud of. I wish that on no man. But just to let you know that's what I witnessed. It's reality. Them niggas was doing their thing. I was just watching. I was a fan of the game. I sat on the porch and watched the Cadillacs go by. The nigga I talk about on my records is Kenneth 'Boobie' Williams."

Ross has also honored Boobie with a DVD profiling the Top 10 urban gangsters and street legends in Miami. Entitled M.I. YAYO, it features the Boobie Boys, Vonda's Gang, The John Doe Boys, Ricky Brownlee, Bunky Brown, and Isaac Hicks. Ross gives an introductory monologue for each segment, and there are interesting interviews throughout with associates of each group. M.I. YAYO is easy to find on YouTube with a simple search and is definitely worth watching.

Through Rick Ross's rap lyrics, Boobie

will live on in infamy, but the glorification of the Boobie Boys has not pleased some members of the gang. Michael "Chico" Harper complained that all the publicity had hurt their chances of winning any type of appeal saying:

"Ross was unconscious of the full effect behind his actions. I know his intentions were good, but it was bad PR for our case. You have niggas still fighting to overturn this shit. It's not a good look when we're arguing the allegations were hyped, distorted and straight up fabricated. But then a nigga with nationwide exposure is constantly trying to validate it with glory. Hip-hop/rap music and its content is so powerful. It travels beyond the realm of our ghetto."

Co-defendant, Arthur "Plex" Pless agreed and said, "Rick Ross is validating what the crackers say by putting it out there. Straight up."[50]

---

[50] All quotes taken from Street Legends, by Seth Ferantti.

Figure 38. Rick Ross wearing his signature Boobie Boys shirt. (Genius.com)

Epilogue

As soon as the guilty verdicts were returned, the North End Task Force was disbanded. My squad went back into the homicide rotation and started picking up fresh murders again.

During the 2½ year tenure of the task force, a total of 63 individuals from both the Boobie Boys and Vonda's Gang were arrested and convicted on federal charges, ranging from narcotics and firearms violations to homicide and drive-by shootings. Over $300,000 in cash was confiscated, and $95,000 in stolen property was recovered. Ten AK-47 rifles and 18 semi-automatic handguns were seized. Thirty-one previously unsolved murders were closed, and leads were developed that led to the closure of 14 additional homicides in Northern Florida, Georgia, North Carolina, and Virginia.

But by far, the most significant accomplishment achieved by the task force was the reduction of the murder rate in the north end of Miami-Dade County by 54 per cent!

Career homicide detectives are always incensed by allegations made by the press and the public that "ghetto murders" are considered insignificant and not taken seriously. The constant implication is that if the victim is black or brown the investigators aren't committed and don't work that hard on the cases. Well, every murder victim in the Boobie Boys case was Black, and in 30 years of police work I have never witnessed a group of cops work harder on any investigation. This case certainly belies that accusation of indifference on the part of homicide detectives when the victims are minorities. Homicide detectives don't care about the color of their victim's skin; they simply do their very best on each and every case.

Jeff Lewis and I continued putting together a CCE case against Vonda in what little spare time we had between homicides. With the help of U.S. Attorneys, Karen Rocklin, Dave Gardey, and Mike Brown, Vonda and five members of her organization were indicted. They were all convicted.

Karen and Mike sought to have Vonda designated a drug kingpin and eligible for the federal death penalty, but the Justice Department in Washington, D. C. refused. Vonda was sentenced to 20 years in federal prison. She was released in 2020.

The North End Task Force received numerous accolades as a result of our efforts. Thomas Scott, the U.S. Attorney for the Southern District of Florida, nominated us to be recipients at the Department of Justice's Directors Ceremony, which was held on November 1, 2001. The presentation took place in the Ronald Reagan Building in Washington, D.C., and we were given the "Outstanding Contributions in Law Enforcement Award" from then Attorney General of the United States, John Ashcroft.

All the members of the North End Task Force are now retired and scattered across the country. Five still live in various parts of Florida. Whenever any of us get together, the conversation invariably turns to the Boobie Boys case. We all refer to it as, "the best case we ever worked, bar none." Between all of us, we have an accumulated 250 years of police experience, but the Boobie Boys investigation will always be remembered as "our finest hour."[51]

To paraphrase Ronald Reagan, "Some people wonder all their lives if they have made a difference or not...we don't have that problem." We can now sit on our porches, in our rocking chairs, knowing that we saved lives, changed history, and put a group of vile killers behind bars. I am honored to have been a part of it. I was privileged to have worked side by side with what was, in my opinion, the best group of investigators ever assembled.

---

[51] From the famous "This was their finest hour" speech given by Winston Churchill.

Figure 39. The entire North End Task Force at a press conference regarding the Boobie Boys. From left to right: Jeff Lewis, Chuck Clark, Dave Simmons, Mike Hernandez, Deputy Director Frank Boni, Carlos Canino, Lenny Athas, Major Jim Loftus, Director Carlos Alvarez, Lt. Tyrone White, the author, Joe Malott, Chris Clark.

Appendix I
DEATH CHART

DATE	VICTIM(S)	STATUS	AFFILIATION
4/22/86	Michael Hollis AKA McBride	Killed	None. By RaRa/Vonda over dope
6/25/86	Jake Brown	Wounded	None. By RaRa/Vonda over dope
6/29/86	Peter Charlston	Wounded	None. By RaRa/Vonda over dope
11/14/87	Gary Coley	Killed	Boobie is arrested for the murder
	Steve Jones	Wounded	of Coley and the attempted
	Victor Fitzpatrick	Wounded	murders of Jones & Fitzpatrick.
5/6/92	Marvin Williams	Wounded	Marvin Williams is Boobies' cousin.
	Dan Johnson	Wounded	
5/27/91	Laverell Johnson	Killed	None. Killed by Boobie and Greylin Kelly over a woman.
9/6/92	Kenneth Williams (Boobie)	Wounded (shot 5 times)	Boobie
11/92	Ruth Russell	Wounded (right leg amputated)	None. Innocent victim
12/25/92	James Powell	Killed	Boobie/Twins
12/30/92	Magnus Hamilton	Killed	Both innocent (killed in attempt on
	Everold Johnson	Killed	Boobie's life)
6/14/93	Harryl Johnson	Killed	Boobie
7/26/93	Sherman Bruce	Wounded	Boobie
8/22/93	Tyrone Leo Florence	Killed	Thomas Family
12/23/93	Roosevelt Davis	Killed	None. Stole dope from E-4
1/6/94	Bernard Shaw	Wounded	Boobie
	Margo Shaw	Wounded	
2/6/94	Alvin Kelly	Killed	None. By E-4's crew over dope territory
2/18/94	Drexel Deveaux	Killed	Dope rip by Boobie Boys
3/10/94	Lavel Mucherson	Wounded	Boobie
	Ozola Hill	Wounded	
3/17/94	Gerry Dukes	Killed	Boobie
	John Hankins	Wounded	
3/17/94	Benny Brownlee	Killed	Thomas Family
3/20/94	Wayne Brownlee	Wounded	Thomas Family
	Aaron Thomas	Wounded	
6/22/94	Walter Betterson	Killed	Thomas Family
	Derrick Harris	Killed	
7/2/94	James Ward	Killed	None. By Boobie Boys over dope
	Marla James	Killed	territory.
8/20/94	Rodney Fullwood	Killed	Thomas Family
9/18/94	Everette Cooper	Killed	None. By E-4's crew over dope territory

11/4/94	Johnny Beliard	killed	None. By E-4's crew over dope territory
3/23/95	Marvin Rogers	Wounded	Boobie
3/24/95	Eddie Davis	Killed	Vonda/RaRa
	Davode McLucas	Killed	
	George Donaldson	Killed	
	Andre McWhorter	Wounded	
5/17/95	Otis Green	Killed	None. By E-4's crew over dope territory.
	Alice Gardner	Killed	
	Michael Frazier (5 yrs.)	Killed	
7/12/95	Carlton Bailey	Killed	Stole dope from Boobie Boys
8/3/95	Ben Johnson	Wounded (paralyzed)	E-4/Boobie
12/12/95	Carlos Ramon	Killed	None. By E-4's crew over dope territory
2/1/96	Ansel Green	Killed	Boobie's cousin
5/19/96	Moses Brown	Killed	None. By E-4's crew over dope territory
5/19/96	Wayne Baptiste	Wounded	Boobie/E-4
	Donald Lorfils	Wounded	
9/24/96	Jesse Swanson	Wounded	Vonda/RaRa
9/26/96	Wallace Fortner	Killed	Vonda/RaRa
10/27/96	Raymond Rich	Killed	Vonda/RaRa
	Rick Delancey	Wounded	
11/5/96	Tarvis Miller	Killed	
12/11/96	Famous Johnson	Wounded	Vonda
	Robert Sawyer	Wounded	
12/25/96	Efrain Casado (E-4)	Wounded	Boobie
	Kinte Hallimon	Wounded	
	Casado's 18-month-old baby	Wounded	
3/22/97	Johnathon Hawthorne (Moose)	Wounded	Boobie & Vonda
3/29/97	Ronald Jones	Killed	Stole drugs from Boobie Boys
4/23/97	Rawn Davis	Killed	By Boobie Boys over dope
5/5/97	Leverraynton Smith	Wounded	John Doe
5/6/97	Laverraynton Smith	Wounded	John Doe
	Damien McCoy	Killed	
7/27/97	Antonio Johnson	Killed	None. By Vonda's crew over dope territory.
8/97	Famous Johnson	Vehicle struck by AK-47 rounds. Neither victim hit.	Vonda
	Robert Sawyer (RaRa)		
10/12/97	Robert Sawyer (RaRa)	Wounded	Vonda
	Yvonne Washington	Wounded	
10/18/97	Curtis "Sissy" Thomas	Wounded	Vonda
11/18/97	Robert Sawyer (Ra Ra)	Wounded	Vonda
	Broderick Jones	Unharmed	
12/6/97	Linard Albury, AKA Shotout		Boobie Boys
	Herbert Clark		
12/31/97	Marvin Rogers	Killed	Boobie

The Boobie Boys: Murder and Mayhem in Miami

1/1/98	Jamal Brown (Pookalotta) Rick Delancey (Kojack)	Wounded (Paralyzed) Wounded	Vonda
1/1/98	Famous Johnson Cedric Smith	Vehicle struck by AK-47 rounds. Neither victim hit.	Vonda/RaRa
2/11/98	Roger Davis Tyrone Tarver	Killed Killed	Vonda
2/22/98	Michael Tyson (Bear)	Killed	Vonda
2/24/98	John Davis	Killed	By the twins over dope territory
4/23/98	Alexander Ray King	Killed	Owed money to Vonda's Gang
5/11/98	Corey Mucherson (Fish Grease)	Killed	Boobie
9/18/98	Leslie Smith (Dune)	Wounded	Boobie
3/19/99	Willie Jones (Billy)	Killed	Boobie and Flave
8/4/01	Josephine Rucker	Killed	Federal witness against Vonda's gang

Appendix II

President John Rivera
Dade County PBA
10680 NW 25 Street
Miami, Florida 33172

RE: Nomination of Homicide Squad K for the PBA Distinguished Service Award.

Dear John:

As a fellow PBA member, I am taking this opportunity to bring to your attention one of the finest examples of dedication to duty, teamwork and tenacious professional police work I have had the pleasure to witness in my 29 years of law enforcement at the state and federal levels.

On February 11, 1998, a group of perpetrators armed with AK-47 rifles committed the double homicide of Tyrone Tarver and Roger Davis. The assailants cut down both victims with a barrage of AK-47 rounds that were indiscriminately fired without regard for innocent bystanders.

During this time period drug related murders were tearing away at the very fabric of life in northern Miami-Dade County. No citizen was immune or secure from danger and armed assaults and homicides had virtually turned the streets into a killing field.

Sergeant Tony Monheim and his squad were tasked with the Herculean directive of ending the violence and set upon their work with the determination and tenacity of a pack of Wolverines. Sgt. Monheim reasoned that extraordinary problems require extraordinary efforts and effectively enlisted the aid of ATF and DEA to exploit all available resources and stem the violence. The Miami-Dade Police Department fully supported the initiative and gave Sgt. Monheim and his entire squad of detectives the green light to follow the case to a successful conclusion.

The trust placed in Sgt. Monheim and his detectives was well founded. In the year and a half that followed, Squad K detectives tirelessly fanned out all over the United States following leads and interviewed in excess of 1,000 witnesses and incarcerated subjects. A historical federal drug trafficking conspiracy case that included 15 murders was pieced together targeting KENNETH WILLIAMS, aka Boobie.

As a result of their efforts, the murder rate in the affected areas has decreased by 54% over the previous year's statistics.

The dedicated efforts of Squad K are an example of keeping in the fine tradition and sense of duty for which the Miami-Dade Police Department is world renowned. The degree of professionalism and tenacity displayed by Squad K should be touted as a national example of what can be achieved when personal agendas are put aside, and everyone pitches in to accomplish a noble goal. A 54% homicide reduction is an achievement worthy of national recognition.

In consideration of the above, I respectfully nominate the following PBA members to your awards committee for formal recognition for a rare and exemplary performance.

Sgt. Tony Monheim
Sgt. Dave Simmons
Det. Jeff Lewis
Det. Mike Hernandez
Det. Joe Malott
Det. Chuck Clark

Sincerely,
W. Leonard Athas

Appendix III
Sources

MESSAGE IS OUT ON BEEPERS
By Jonathan M. Moses
July 11, 1988
https://www.washingtonpost.com/archive/politics/198
8/07/11/message-is-out-on-beepers/58840caa-523

The Beeper, the Pay Phone and the DEA's 'Operation Dinero':
BY PAUL LIEBERMAN
JAN. 7, 1995
https://www.latimes.com/archives/la-xpm-1995-01-07-
me-17316-story.htmle-413b-9224-60ad94d7803f/

For Barnhart, it's always been about the practice
By Alice Reese Herald-Banner Contributor Sep 20, 2021
https://www.heraldbanner.com/news/local_news/for-
barnhart-its-always-been-about-the-
practice/article_7f7be8f0-1960-11ec-b08d-
e3843cb83a0e.html

UPI ARCHIVES JULY 25, 1997
Murder defendant attacked in court
https://www.upi.com/Archives/1997/07/25/Murder-
defendant-attacked-in-court/9175869803200/

United States Court of Appeals, Eleventh Circuit.
Jason Demetrius STEPHENS, Petitioner–Appellant, v.
SECRETARY, FLORIDA DEPARTMENT OF
CORRECTIONS, Attorney General, State of Florida,
Respondents–Appellees.
No. 11–11727.

Forensic Science Online
An Introduction Forensic Firearms Identification
https://www.firearmsid.com/A_FirearmsID.htm

Miami New Times
Rolex vs. Rollexx
CALVIN GODFREY
JANUARY 18, 2007

13 PEOPLE CHARGED IN MULTISTATE CRACK RING
By ROGER CHESLEY Daily Press
Apr 25, 1998.
https://www.dailypress.com/news/dp-xpm-19980425-
1998-04-25-9804250124-story.html

NEW TIMES
Our Hero the Drug Dealer
TRISTRAM KORTEN APRIL 23, 1998 4:00AM
https://www.miaminewtimes.com/news/our-hero-the-
drug-dealer-6366918?showFullText=true

Cocaine Cowboys: How to Make Crack
https://vimeo.com/1611326

Miami Herald
Miami Cocaine Prices Soar
October 5, 2020
By David Ovalle
https://miamiherald.newspapers.com/image/legacy/6862
79871/?terms=Miami%20cocaine%20prices%20soar&mat
ch=1

Encyclopedia Britannica

Crack Epidemic
By Deonna S. Turner
https://www.britannica.com/topic/crack-epidemic

Hat Trick: Trick Daddy Files For 3rd Bankruptcy Just Before Foreclosure
Written By Alvin Aqua Blanco
Posted May 21, 2017
https://hiphopwired.com/544056/hat-trick-trick-daddy-files-3rd-bankruptcy-just-foreclosure/

ET
Trina to Receive the 'I Am Hip Hop Award' at 2022 BET Hip Hop Awards
By Mekishana Pierre, September 22, 2022
https://www.etonline.com/trina-to-receive-the-i-am-hip-hop-award-at-2022-bet-hip-hop-awards-191400

American Gun Facts
The story of the Chinese AK-47
https://americangunfacts.com/norinco-mak-90/

The Miami Herald
Shooting Suspect Sought
By Joan Fleishman
June 30, 1986

M.I. Yayo
https://www.youtube.com/watch?v=RMB3IpwnE3g

Eagles' Jervonte Jackson Dreams of Freedom for his Mom
May 22, 2009
https://www.inquirer.com/philly/hp/sports/20090522_Eagles__Jervonte_Jackson_dreams_of_freedom_for_his_m

om.html

Man Dies After Neighborhood Rampage
By Patrick May
April 25, 1989
https://miamiherald.newspapers.com/image/634834043/?
terms=benjamin%20bryant&match=1

*STUDIO 183: THREE HOT ATTRACTIONS, ONE
SMART PROPRIETOR*
By JOHN LANNERT
South Florida Sun-Sentinel
Mar 15, 1991
https://www.sun-sentinel.com/news/fl-xpm-1991-03-15-
9101130666-story.html

Tampa Bay Times
Miami trauma center leads in care of gunshot wounds
Published Oct. 13, 1993 | Updated Oct. 10, 2005
https://www.tampabay.com/archive/1993/10/13/miami-
trauma-center-leads-in-care-of-gunshot-wounds/

Shots, Death on the Palmetto
By Gail Epstein
March 25, 1995
https://miamiherald.newspapers.com/image/640069126/?
terms=devode&match=1

DiMaio, Vincent. *Gunshot Wounds*. New York, CRC
Press, 1999.

Wright, Evan. *How To Get Away With Murder In America*,
Amazon Digital Publishing, 2015.

The Miami Herald
Man accused of scalding wife.
By Luisa Yanez
March 21, 2004
https://miamiherald.newspapers.com/image/650418175/?
terms=tomas%20casado&match=1

What Are the Types and Degrees of Burns?
Written by WebMD Editorial Contributors
 Medically Reviewed by Carol DerSarkissian, MD on
April 14, 2021
https://www.webmd.com/first-aid/types-degrees-burns

The MAC-10
https://en.wikipedia.org/wiki/MAC-10

Jason Stephens Florida Death Row
BY MYCRIMELIBRARY.COM / ON APRIL 7, 2021
https://mycrimelibrary.com/jason-stephens-florida-
death-row/

The Miami Herald, 21 Oct 1966
Indictments Net Two more: Veteran Officer and Ex-Convict
by Karl Wickstrom
https://miamiherald.newspapers.com/image/621888311/?
terms=Manson%20Hill

The Miami Herald, 25 Feb 1998, Wed · Page 20
One Person Dies in North Dade Robbery

The Miami Herald, 14 Mar 1964.
Bracelet Quiz Lie Tests Out

By Gene Miller
https://miamiherald.newspapers.com/image/620532563/?
terms=Manson%20Hill%20%2B%20tropical&match=1

Murderpedia: Robert Frederick Carr III.
https://murderpedia.org/male.C/c/carr-robert-
frederick.htm

Carr: Five Years of Rape and Murder by Edna Buchanan.
https://www.amazon.com/Carr-Five-Years-Rape-
Murder

The Miami Herald, 10 May 1998, Sun
Deadly Gang Wars by Gail Epstein
https://miamiherald.newspapers.com/image/642164044/

*6 Common Federal Crimes with Mandatory Minimum Prison
Sentences*
Posted By: Staff Writer
https://www.johntfloyd.com/6-common-federal-crimes-
with-mandatory-minimum-prison-
sentences/#:~:text=Some%20federal%20crimes%20carry
%20a,without%20the%20benefit%20of%20parole.

UNITED STATES SENTENCING COMMISSION
ONE COLUMBUS CIRCLE, N.E.
WASHINGTON, DC 20002
https://www.ussc.gov/sites/default/files/pdf/research-
and-publications/research-
publications/2016/Rule35b.pdf

Suspected member of drug gang killed in Titusville.
The Miami Herald
By Gail Epstein

May 12, 1998

Dade Lawyer: I didn't tamper with witnesses
By Gail Epstein
August 28, 2000
https://miamiherald.newspapers.com/article/the-miami-herald/125184609/

Only witness to slaying found dead.
By Adam Ramirez
The Miami Herald
30 Jul 1997, Wed · Page 19

The Port of Miami
https://en.wikipedia.org/wiki/PortMiami

United States v. Stitt
https://caselaw.findlaw.com/court/us-4th-circuit/1231686.html

The Unites States Marshals
https://en.wikipedia.org/wiki/United_States_Marshals_Service

Judge Kevin Michael Moore
https://en.wikipedia.org/wiki/Kevin_Michael_Moore#:~:text=Moore%20was%20nominated%20by%20President,commission%20on%20February%2010%2C%201992.

The Miami Herald
16 Aug 2001, Thu · Page A2
Moore a law and order judge
https://miamiherald.newspapers.com/image/669359879/?terms=judge%20k.%20michael%20moore

RESERVING OUR STATE'S LEGAL HERITAGE:
RESTORATION OF THE HISTORIC MIAMI
COURTROOM 6-1
FLORIDA BAR JOURNAL
Vol. 83, No. 7 July/August 2009 Maria S. Johnson

Chepesiuk, Ron. *Gangsters of Miami*, Fort Lee, Barricade
Press, 2010

Chepesiuk, Ron. Queenpins, Rock Hill, Strategic Medial
Books, 2012

Steet Kings of Miami, Seth Ferranti, Gorilla Convict
Publications, 2015.

A Tribute to Tobacco Road
https://tobacco-road.com/

ABOUT THE AUTHOR

Tony Monheim retired from the Miami-Dade Police Department in 2004, after a distinguished, 30-year career. He was assigned to the Homicide Bureau as a squad supervisor during the final 12 years of his tenure. Prior to that, he spent 16 years in the Robbery Bureau as both an investigator and a supervisor.

He holds a master's degree in public administration from St. Thomas of Villanova University and a bachelor's degree from Western Illinois University, where he was a standout rugby player. He has been afforded expert witness status in both Federal and State (Florida) court regarding homicide investigative procedures. He has written numerous articles on homicide and investigative techniques for law enforcement publications and is the author of another true crime book entitled, I Have A Devil Inside Me.

Printed in Great Britain
by Amazon